THE WASTE LAND

A Facsimile and Transcript of the Original Drafts

T. S. ELIOT

THE WASTE LAND

A FACSIMILE AND TRANSCRIPT OF THE ORIGINAL DRAFTS INCLUDING THE ANNOTATIONS OF EZRA POUND

EDITED BY

VALERIE ELIOT

A HARVEST BOOK
HARCOURT BRACE & COMPANY
SAN DIEGO NEW YORK LONDON

Library of Congress Cataloging-in-Publication Data
Eliot, T. S. (Thomas Stearns), 1888–1965.
The waste land: a facsimile and transcript of the original drafts
including the annotations of Ezra Pound/edited by Valerie Eliot.
p. cm. — (A Harvest book)
Includes bibliographical references
ISBN 0-15-694870-2
I. Eliot, Valerie. II. Title.
PS3509.L43W3 1994
821′.912—dc20 94-16082

Printed in the United States of America

F G H I J

CONTENTS

PREFACE

THE more we know of Eliot, the better. I am thankful that the lost leaves have been unearthed.

The occultation of 'The Waste Land' manuscript (years of waste time, exasperating to its author) is pure Henry James.

'The mystery of the missing manuscript' is now solved. Valerie Eliot has done a scholarly job which would have delighted her husband. For this, and for her patience with my attempts to elucidate my own marginal notes, and for the kindness which distinguishes her, I express my thanks.

EZRA POUND

Venice
30 September 1969

The facsimile of the original manuscript of *The Waste Land* is reproduced herewith through the courtesy of the Henry W. and Albert A. Berg Collection of English and American Literature in The New York Public Library, Astor, Lenox, and Tilden Foundations.

INTRODUCTION

1915 'A young chap named Eliot has gone back to America for a bit. I have more or less discovered him', wrote Ezra Pound to John Quinn on 12 August. 'I wish you'd drop him a post card and tell him where he can see you . . . I have every confidence in his discretion . . . He has more entrails than might appear from his quiet exterior, I think.'[1] But Eliot's brief visit to discuss his plans with his parents was over before contact could be made, and he never met the New York lawyer, patron, and art collector[2] to whom he gave the manuscript of *The Waste Land* in gratitude for having done so much to protect and further his interests.

The dissertation[3] for a doctorate in philosophy which Eliot began while a student in the Harvard Graduate School, from October 1911 until June 1914, was continued at Oxford when he was given a Sheldon Travelling Fellowship to study Aristotle for a year under Harold Joachim. Towards the end of his period at Merton College, he confided his dilemma to Conrad Aiken: Harvard had renominated him to his Fellowship, but he did not enjoy Oxford. If he could be allowed to stay in London and work at the British Museum, he would be content, though he did not think he would ever come to like England; on the other hand, he dreaded returning to Cambridge [Massachusetts] 'and the College bell, and the people whom one fights against and who absorb one all the same'.[4]

Shrewdly realizing that his future as a writer lay in England, Pound encouraged him to settle there, and to marry an Englishwoman, Vivien Haigh-Wood, which he did after leaving Oxford in June. In the same month, at Pound's insistence, *The Love-Song of J. Alfred Prufrock* appeared in *Poetry*.

To please his parents, who were distressed by his decision to live abroad, and because he felt he owed it to Harvard, Eliot agreed to finish his thesis while teaching in the autumn term at High Wycombe Grammar School, where the salary was £140 per annum with dinner. The immediate problem, as he explained to his father on 10 September, was money: '. . . until January we shall be in urgent need of funds . . . we have planned a very economical way of life, and Vivien's resourcefulness and forethought are inexhaustible'. It was not a question of trying to make living easier, 'but how to live at all'. And again, on the 27th, 'I should, but for the degree, have devoted my spare time to writing, which would have pieced out my income.'

[1] Eliot and Pound met in London on 22 September 1914.

[2] See *The Man from New York: John Quinn and His Friends*, by B. L. Reid (1968).

[3] *Knowledge and Experience in the Philosophy of F. H. Bradley* (1963).

[4] 25 February.

Apart from *Preludes* and *Rhapsody on a Windy Night* (in the second issue of Wyndham Lewis's *Blast*), Eliot's poetry had been printed in American magazines, and Pound was determined to introduce it to London. With this aim he made a selection of poems from Yeats to the Imagists which was published by Elkin Mathews in November as *Catholic Anthology*. Eliot's contributions were *Prufrock*, *Portrait of a Lady*, *The Boston Evening Transcript*, *Miss Helen Slingsby*, and a new piece, *Hysteria*.

1916 In January Eliot moved to a better post at Highgate Junior School which brought him £160 per annum with dinner and tea, and he began to rewrite his thesis. His wife had been very ill, he told Aiken on the 10th; his friend Jean Verdenal had been killed; *Catholic Anthology* had not done very well 'in spite of the name of Yeats'; and he had been so 'taken up with the worries of finance and Vivien's health' that he had 'written nothing lately. I *hope* to write when I have more detachment. But I am having a wonderful time nevertheless. I have *lived* through material for a score of long poems in the last six months. An entirely different life from that I looked forward to two years ago. Cambridge seems to me a dull nightmare now. . . .'

Pound and Quinn were planning a New York Exhibition of the work of the Vorticists, and when Wyndham Lewis objected to his paintings being consigned to one ship 'in these torpedoing times',[1] Pound suggested that Eliot should carry half the items in his luggage when he sailed to America on 1 April to take his *viva* at Harvard. He asked Quinn to send a clerk to meet Eliot at the dock and see him through customs; he undertook to attend to details such as an extra trunk at this end. When the boat was withdrawn at short notice, however, Eliot decided to forgo his doctorate, although his thesis was accepted towards it.

> The school takes up most of my days, and in my spare (sic) time I have been writing: philosophy for the *Monist* and the *International Journal of Ethics*, reviews for the *New Statesman*, the *Manchester Guardian* and the *Westminster Gazette*. . . . I am now trying to get an introduction to the *Nation* . . . I have reviewed some good books and much trash. It is good practice in writing, and teaches one speed both in reading and writing. It is bad in this way, that one acquires an extraordinary appetite for volumes, and exults at the mass of printed matter which one has devoured and evacuated. I crave a new book every few days. . . . Composing on the typewriter, I find that I am sloughing off all my long sentences which I used to dote upon. Short, staccato, like modern French prose. The typewriter makes for lucidity, but I am not sure that it encourages subtlety.
>
> This autumn will find me busier than ever, as I am preparing a set of six lectures on contemporary intellectual movements in France to deliver under the auspices of Oxford to the general public—mostly, I believe, ladies. If they come off, I ought to be able to secure plenty of lecturing, at least enough to keep us.[2]

Vivien's health had been

a great anxiety all winter and spring, as she kept having incidental troubles like teeth which set

[1] Pound to Quinn, 9 March. [2] To Conrad Aiken, 21 August.

her back . . . It has been nerves, complicated by physical ailments, and induced largely by the most acute neuralgia . . . We are vegetating and gaining health against the coming term on a backwater near Portsmouth Harbour [Bosham], where the tide is either very much in or very much out; the place alternates between mud and water, and is very charming. I have been working always in the mornings, and bathing, boating and bicycling in the afternoon.[1]

He admitted that

I often feel that *J. A[lfred] P[rufrock]* is a swan-song, but I never mention the fact because Vivien is so exceedingly anxious that I shall equal it, and would be bitterly disappointed if I do not. . . . The present year has been, in some respects, the most awful nightmare of anxiety that the mind of man could conceive, but at least it is not dull, and it has its compensations.[2]

I have certainly reason to be proud of my family; the way they have accepted the responsibility of helping me, without a single murmur has been wonderful. . . . I hope that a year from now I may be self-supporting. I am basing most of the hope on lectures, of course. You know that I am giving up the school at Christmas, as I find that I am losing in every way. I have not time to pursue my literary connections, and overwork is telling on the quality of my production. After Christmas, I hope to see people and drum up trade.[3]

1917 Thankful to be done with 'the smell of school books', Eliot was dependent on what he could earn from lecturing and reviewing, and he wrote somewhat defensively to his father

. . . the war has blocked the best possible opportunities and openings. If anything else had done it I might not feel justified in going on; if there had been no opportunities or openings, or if I had proved incompetent to make the most of them. But this has not been the case; setting the war aside, I have succeeded in what I have undertaken. And the opportunities are still there, and I feel justified in waiting for them, and not chucking away all the capital of work that I have put into them, and which will remain good to my credit if I can hang on to it. This is why I feel justified in hanging on through the rest of the war with any employment I can get.[4]

After 'hunting for work to stop the gap', he was, by 21 March, 'in much better spirits than I have been for some time past' because a friend[5] of the Haigh-Woods had given him an introduction to Lloyds Bank, where he was earning two pounds ten shillings a week filing and tabulating balance sheets of foreign banks 'in such a way as to show the progress or decline of every bank from year to year'. He enjoyed his employment, which was more interesting and less fatiguing than teaching; his French and Italian were invaluable, and he would have to acquire a little Spanish, Danish, Swedish, and Norwegian. While the salary was not princely, there were good prospects of a rise as he gained experience, and after five o'clock he was free to think about his Class or his writing.

[1] Ibid.

[2] To his brother, Henry, 6 September.

[3] Idem, 6 November.

[4] 1 March.

[5] He began work in the Colonial and Foreign Department of Lloyds Bank on 19 March, having been recommended by the late Mr. L. E. Thomas, who was the Chief General Manager of the National Provincial Bank.

It was satisfying to have a regular occupation, and he would be able to do his own work 'much the better for it'.[1]

I want to find out something about the science of money while I am at it: it is an extraordinarily interesting subject. Vivien was very anxious about my health while I was at home—it seemed to get worse and worse; and now I am better and more cheerful she is much happier. Then too I have felt more creative lately. Besides my lectures,[2] which are now on Ruskin and involve some reading in political economy, and considerable reviewing for Jourdain (mostly anthropology and biology lately), I have been doing some writing—mostly in French, curiously enough it has taken me that way. . . .[3]

When Richard Aldington joined the army, Eliot succeeded him (through Pound's advocacy) as assistant editor of the *Egoist*, at a salary of nine pounds a quarter, to which Pound secretly contributed.

Since the previous April, when he had helped Eliot to select the poems for his first volume, Pound had been urging a reluctant Elkin Mathews to undertake publication. Finally, because the latter 'was fussing about cost of paper, etc., and risk, and wanting part expenses paid', Pound explained to Quinn, '. . . I told him if he wouldn't publish . . . without fuss, someone else would. *The Egoist* is doing it. That is *officially* The Egoist. As a matter of fact I have borrowed the cost of the printing bill (very little) and am being the Egoist. But Eliot don't [*sic*] know it, nor does anyone else save my wife, and Miss Weaver of The Egoist [the two lenders] & it is not for public knowledge.'[4] Quinn offered to stand the charge, but Pound was confident that the book would pay its way. Five hundred copies of *Prufrock and Other Observations* were published in June, and on the 12th Pound proposed to Alfred Knopf that he should bring out an American edition. Quinn also drew the publisher's attention to the book when he sent him a copy early in August, with the comment that he liked everything about it except the title. 'I do not know whether it is great poetry or not', Knopf replied. 'I do know that it is great fun and I like it.' But he considered the thirty-two pages too few; there was nothing he could do with such a small collection 'except to give it away as an advertisement. And even that would be difficult.'[5]

Knopf approved of Quinn's idea that a brochure should be printed on Pound's work in order to make it more widely known. Choosing Eliot to write it, Pound ruled that it should be issued anonymously: 'I want to boom Eliot and one cant have too obvious a ping-pong match at that sort of thing'.[6] When the text was ready in September, Pound made three deletions and provided the title: *Ezra Pound: His Metric and Poetry.*

Without delay, Eliot switched to another task:

I have begun to be very busy the last few days preparing my lectures. One set covers very much

[1] To his Mother, 21 March.

[2] His Monday evening Tutorial Class for working people gave him 'immense pleasure'.

[3] To his Mother, 11 April.

[4] 11 April.

[5] To Quinn, 17 August.

[6] Idem, 11 April.

> the same ground as my lectures at Southall last year, but more broadly, beginning with 'The Makers of 19th Century Ideas', lectures on Carlyle, Mill, Arnold, Huxley, Spencer, Ruskin, Morris—then the poets, and then the novelists. . . . The other course is a continuation of last year's; they want me to start with Emerson, go on to Samuel Butler and William Morris, then the Pre-Raphaelites, and so on. Both of these courses depend for their continuance upon the enrolment at the first few lectures, so I am waiting anxiously.[1]

They were soon assured, 'as enough members have enrolled for each; whereat I am much rejoiced, as it is rather a compliment to a class to exist at all at the present time, and also we shall need the money very much this winter.'[2] There were disadvantages: lecturing took more out of him than the bank did during the day, and consumed time that he wanted to spend on writing of a less ephemeral nature.

Against his wishes, Vivien had been seeking a place in a government office, only to find that being married to an American was

> a complete bar. I am only sorry because I am afraid she will now want to look elsewhere, and would take something where the people are less agreeable and the hours longer. . . . I do not think she could stand the sort of work she would be given to do in a bank; the hours are too long, she would have to arrive at the same time every day in spite of sleepless nights and headaches. . . . It would be much harder on her than on me, even if she had my health. . . .[3]

> . . . everyone's individual lives are so swallowed up in the one great tragedy that one almost ceases to have personal experiences or emotions, and such as one has seem so unimportant, where before it would have seemed interesting even to tell about a lunch of bread and cheese. It's only very dull people who feel they have more in their lives now—other people have too much. I have a lot of things to write about if the time ever comes when people will attend to them.[4]

1918 I am told by Pound that you expressed satisfaction with the brochure on his work [Eliot said to Quinn on 4 March]. I am very glad if this is so, because I wrote it under considerable pressure of time, and was very much aware of its shortcomings. I lamented not being able to have sight of the proofs. I only hope that it will serve the desired purpose, and shall be very glad if it induces any one unacquainted with Pound's stuff to buy and read his books.

Quinn had investigated a rumour that Boni & Liveright intended to pirate *Prufrock*, and was able to notify Eliot that it was unfounded, being merely 'a mare's nest stirred up by [the Editors of *The Little Review*] who jumped to the conclusion and told me as a fact what they only suspected'.[5] Thanking him for his kindness, Eliot continued: 'I appreciated it the more because I knew you had recently undergone a serious operation; I do not think that there are many people who, under such conditions, would

[1] To his Mother, 12 September.

[2] Idem, 14 October. His second course entailed giving twenty-five lectures on 'Victorian Literature' on Friday evenings from 7 to 9 o'clock.

[3] Idem, 15 November.

[4] To his Father, 23 December.

[5] 19 April.

bestir themselves so actively even for personal friends, still less for a man who was personally unknown to them.'

He was afraid it would be some time before he could really expect to double his slim book, and make it of a suitable size for the American public, because 'I have only written half a dozen small poems in the last year, and the last I have been unable to finish. I regret still more that I have been unable to do anything this winter for *The Little Review*.' He spent a 'sufficiently fatiguing day in a bank', gave two evening lectures a week 'involving considerable preparation', and had his editorial duties in connection with the *Egoist*, all of which left him without time or energy for original work.

He hoped to have leisure when his current lectures ended at Easter. 'My Southall people want to do Elizabethan Literature next year which would interest me more than what we have done before, and would be of more use to me too, as I want to write some essays on the dramatists who have never been properly criticised.'[1]

Eliot throve on the hot weather of late May and early June: 'I have written several poems lately[2] and wrote a review today of three philosophy books for *The New Statesman*.'[3] Both he and Vivien were in poor health after the winter and his doctor advised him to spend the summer in the country. They picked Marlow.

> We are staying . . . in the street where Shelley used to live. I feel much better already, mentally and physically. The relief of being out of London, getting quite away from it at the end of the day, is very great. The train journey is restful too. . . . I think I am a little fatter—you know I have lost 15 lbs since leaving Oxford. . . . I have been sitting out in a back garden all day writing about Henry James and Hawthorne.[4] The roses are wonderful.[5]

By September Eliot had a book 'almost ready' for Knopf, consisting of a miscellany of prose (mostly critical) and verse (including *Prufrock*). He would have preferred 'to keep the prose and verse apart', especially as the former bore 'marks of haste in the writing in many places. But it is time I had a volume in America, and this is the only way to do it; and Pound's [*Pavannes and Divisions*] will provide a precedent. I hope you will not find [mine] a wholly journalistic compilation.'[6]

It was Pound who made the final adjustments to the manuscript before sending it to the publisher, because Eliot was preoccupied with trying to find some way in which he could be useful to the country. Having been rejected for active service owing to a congenital hernia and tachycardia, he applied to the Intelligence branch of the United States Navy, only to discover that he would have to enlist as a seaman and take an examination in a number of subjects. This was too slow and uncertain, so he turned his

[1] To his Mother, 10 May.

[2] *Sweeney among the Nightingales*, *Whispers of Immortality*, *Dans le restaurant*, *Mr. Eliot's Sunday Morning Service*. Published as 'Four Poems' in the *Little Review*, v. 5 (September 1918), 10–14.

[3] Published, unsigned, as 'New Philosophers' in the *New Statesman*, xi. 275 (13 July 1918), 296–7.

[4] Published as 'The Hawthorne Aspect [of Henry James]' in the *Little Review*, v. 4 (August 1918), 47–53.

[5] To his Mother, 9 June.

[6] To Quinn, 8 September.

attention to the Army, where the Quartermaster Corps had been suggested. No sooner had he collected about sixteen 'excellent' recommendations from various English officials, than he ran into a lieutenant engaged in starting a Political Intelligence section, who was quite sure that Eliot was the man he wanted, and asked him to delay his application until he had seen his chief who was due in London shortly. A week or so later, Eliot heard that Washington had cancelled the project. He was referred next to a major in charge of the ordinary Army Intelligence, who thought he would obtain a commission if he could provide at least three American testimonials in addition to the English ones. Backed by Pound, Eliot looked to Quinn for support, which came by cable and letter to the authorities.

Yet he was to remain a civilian. 'My vicissitudes in connection with the Army and Navy have been surprising. Everything turned to red tape in my hands', Eliot related to Quinn on 13 November. Just as he had secured the necessary testimonials

> I was *sent for* by the Navy Intelligence, who said that I had been mentioned to them as the most suitable man available for certain work of theirs, and . . . that if I could join them as soon as possible they would make me a Chief Yeoman and raise me to a commission in a few months. I accordingly abandoned the Army, arranged to leave the bank, and told the Navy that I would come to enrol in two weeks. When I did so they were not ready—they had cabled to Washington, as they said they had to do in any case, as a matter of routine, (though they had not mentioned this fact in the first place) and not received an answer. So I waited about a week, having left the bank. Then they sent word to me that the permission was received, so I went to enrol, and had commenced this ceremony before they discovered that as I had already registered for Military Service (as all citizens are supposed to) they did not have sufficient authority. I pointed out that *all* citizens of military age were registered, or if not that they lost their American rights and were automatically absentees from the British Army, but it was no use, they cabled again. After I had hung about in this way for two weeks, out of a job, I decided that I could not stand the financial loss . . . and returned to the bank.

> The Lloyds managers were very sympathetic and delighted to have me back. So they signed an appeal for my exemption and I started to learn some new and more intricate work, and two days later the armistice was signed. . . . The experiences I have been through have been paralysing. It has been just like a chancery suit—dragging on and on, and always apparently about to end.[1]

> I think [Vivien] is on the whole stronger than she was. . . . The doctor still prescribes a very careful and regular life for her, and she still has bad migraines whenever she worries or over-exerts herself. I do not understand it, and it worries me.[2]

He implied that his health had improved; according to Pound it was 'in a very shaky state. Doctor orders him not to write any prose for six months.'[3]

1919 'I have heard nothing at all from Knopf about my MS. I cabled him a week ago, or Pound cabled for me. Knopf must have had the MS for over two months, but he has

[1] To his Mother, 13 November. [2] Idem, 22 December. [3] To Quinn, 27 December.

not acknowledged receipt, so I have been worried', Eliot complained to Quinn on 6 January.

> I am not at all proud of the book—the prose part consists of articles written under high pressure in the overworked, distracted existence of the last two years, and [is] very rough in form. But it is important to me that it should be published for private reasons. I am coming to America to visit my family some time within the summer or autumn, and I should particularly like to have it appear first. You see I settled over here in the face of strong family opposition, on the claim that I found the environment more favourable to the production of literature. This book is all I have to show for my claim—it would go toward making my parents contented with conditions and toward satisfying them that I have not made a mess of my life, as they are inclined to believe.

On the 26th he imparted that:

> . . . my father has died, but this does not weaken the need for a book at all—it really reinforces it—my mother is still alive. . . . If you could write or speak to Knopf and find out his definite intentions, I should be very grateful. If he intends to use the stuff I should like him to get busy on it; if not, I should like him to deliver it into your hands. Perhaps then you could look it over with a view to what publisher might be willing to take it? Really you are the only person I know in New York to whom I would entrust such an affair, and I hope you will not think me very cheeky in proposing it. And of course I don't know that you are not either in very poor health or very overworked, or both. But a great deal hangs on it for me, and it was already a pressing matter several months ago!

At the end of January Knopf informed Pound that he was rejecting both his and Eliot's manuscripts,[1] and when they were received by Quinn a fortnight later, he sent them to Boni & Liveright. On 29 April Quinn told Eliot that Pound's book, *Instigations*, had been accepted, but his own was still under consideration. And he commented that Knopf 'would like to publish your poems alone but not the poems with the prose'. Eliot wrote on 25 May that he wished to alter the manuscript if it were possible, as he had two or three essays and a very few poems (including *Gerontion*) to add, and the essays, from the *Athenaeum*, were better than those submitted. Quinn cabled him to send what he had and on the same day, 30 June, expressed his anger with Liveright who, he believed, had delayed his answer because he knew the lawyer was about to go on holiday, and hoped to force him to accept his terms at the last minute: '. . . Liveright expected me to put up a guaranty of $100 or $150 in connection with your book. If he had been decent about it, I should have been willing to do so.' Having retrieved the manuscript, Quinn arranged for it to be offered (with a $150 advance) to John Lane; apologizing for the delay, they replied early in August: 'Mr. Eliot's work is no doubt brilliant, but it is not exactly the kind of material we care to add to our list.' Then Quinn contacted Knopf, who 'was willing and anxious to publish the poems in a volume by

[1] 'Knopf wrote to Pound that the success of his book *Pavannes and Divisions* had not been sufficient to warrant his undertaking any new contracts with him, Wyndham Lewis or myself.' Eliot to Henry Eliot, 27 February.

themselves' now that their number had increased. Both men disliked the name *Prufrock* —which they believed would damage the sales—and decided that the title should be *Poems by T. S. Eliot*.

'It is quite obvious that without you, I should never get anything published in America at all', Eliot had written to Quinn on 9 July.

Earlier in the year, John Middleton Murry had offered Eliot the assistant editorship of the *Athenaeum* at £500 per annum. Although flattered, he declined the invitation for several reasons, perhaps the most important of which was that he

> felt that the constant turning out of 'copy' for a weekly paper would exhaust me for genuine creative work. It would *never* be my first interest, any more than finance is. Finance I can get away from at the end of a day, but review writing would stay by me. I should always be toiling to make my work better than it need be for ephemeral reading. I could not turn it out mechanically and then go to my own work.[1]

When Miss Weaver and Miss Marsden decided to suspend publication of the *Egoist*, Eliot felt robbed of a medium where he could express himself editorially; he was aware that 'other publications cut into the *Egoist* to a certain extent, and the small public which *I* could bring to it now reads the *Athenaeum* every week. There I am a sort of white boy; I have a longish critical review about three weeks out of four, but don't write editorials. It has brought me a certain notoriety which I should never have got from the *Egoist*.'[2] And it brought him a request from Bruce Richmond to write occasional leading articles for *The Times Literary Supplement*.

In May, *Poems 1919* was published by Leonard and Virginia Woolf at the Hogarth Press, and Eliot's three years' course of lectures ended. He went to France for his holiday in mid-August, as it was 'certain to set me up. The relief of getting into another country after five years in one spot and being able to speak another language is a great stimulus and tonic.'[3] Part of the time he spent with Pound in the village of Excideuil in the Dordogne, and part on walking trips alone.

On 3 October Quinn sent Knopf's contract in which he had made a few amendments before signing it as Eliot's attorney. 'I was glad that I was able to dispose of this matter today . . . so that now my part in connection with launching your book is finished. It is a satisfaction to me to feel that I have been of some assistance to you for, as you know, I am a great admirer of your work and I believe that you have a very distinguished future in the world of letters.' Eliot replied: 'I earnestly hope that my affairs will not take any more of your time and thought; if you took no further interest in them whatever you would still have earned my lifelong gratitude, which, I assure you, you shall have.'

In the last paragraph of this letter, written on 5 November, came the first mention

[1] To his Mother, 29 March.
[2] To Quinn, 9 July.
[3] To Henry Eliot, 14 September.

of *The Waste Land*: 'I am now at work on an article ordered by *The Times*,[1] and when that is off I hope to get started on a poem I have in mind.'

His New Year's Resolution, he told his mother on 18 December, 'is to write a long poem I have had on my mind for a long time . . .'.

1920 When *Poems by T. S. Eliot* was published by Knopf on 18 February, nearly a month earlier than promised, Quinn bought thirty-five copies. 'I read [the book] aloud on two evenings to friends of mine, and made converts of both', Eliot learned. 'It is one of the most original notes that has been struck since Synge published his best work, and . . . it has more intellect than Synge.'[2] Several days after the same collection (except that *Ode* replaced *Hysteria*) had come out in London in a limited edition under the title *Ara Vos Prec*, Eliot wrote to his brother about it: 'Some of the new poems, the Sweeney ones, especially *Among the Nightingales* and *Burbank*, are intensely serious, and I think these two are among the best that I have ever done. But even here I am considered by the ordinary newspaper critic as a wit or satirist, and in America I suppose I shall be thought merely disgusting.'[3]

Eliot yearned for a visit from his mother, who felt that she ought not to leave America until her husband's affairs were in order.

> I am thinking all the time of my desire to see her. I cannot get away from it. Unless I can really *see* her again I shall never be happy. Now if I come to America it will be nothing but haste, worry, and fatigue. I can get, at most, ten or possibly fourteen days with her. We should be thinking of the end the whole time. Vivien could not come with me because of the cost of the fare, and mother would never see her. Mother and I would both be simply worn out by it (and of course, it would be my only holiday for a year). Now why should not mother come here while she is physically able, and keep my visits to America until *she* is no longer strong enough to come?[3]

Eliot's salary had risen to five hundred pounds. He had been put in charge of settling all the pre-War Debts between the Bank and Germans, 'an important appointment, full of interesting legal questions',[4] and he was kept busy 'trying to elucidate knotty points in that appalling document the Peace Treaty'.[5] The respect in which he was held by his colleagues was indicated by a high official who told him 'that when some of the men who returned from the War presented a petition against the advancement of newer men over their heads, they made an exception of my case'.[6]

Pound expressed his concern for Eliot in a letter to Quinn on 4 June:

> No use blinking the fact that it is a crime against literature to let him waste eight hours vitality per diem in that bank.

[1] 'Ben Jonson', *The Times Literary Supplement*, London, 930 (13 November 1919), [637]–638. An unsigned review of *Ben Jonson* by G. Gregory Smith.

[2] 6 March.

[3] 15 February.

[4] To his Mother, 15 February.

[5] Idem, 21 February.

[6] Idem, 6 January.

Nor on the other hand that it will take £400 per year, with 3 or 5 years guarantee to get him out of it.

(His wife hasn't a cent and is an invalid always cracking up, & needing doctors, & incapable of earning anything—though she has tried . . .)

Was there any chance, Pound asked, 'of raising this sum from four or five people who wd. keep their mouths shut'? He thought he might be able to give £50 in the first year and perhaps for a further two years if he was still retained by the magazines for which he wrote: 'Though Eliot would have to be kept damn well in ignorance of where that particular £50 was coming from. The boy hasn't got my constitution, certain sorts of prolific outpourings can't (thank god) be expected of him. It is a question of saving three or four books like his vol. of poems from remaining in the limbo of not getting written.' Willing to donate £50 a year for three years, Quinn was not prepared to find other subscribers, and when, subsequently, the *New Age* and the *Athenaeum* ceased to employ Pound as a critic, the plan had to be dropped.

Eliot, who was troubled about Pound, sought Quinn's

candid and confidential opinion about [him] and his future. . . . The fact is that there is now no organ of any importance in which he can express himself, and he is becoming forgotten. It is not enough for him simply to publish a volume of verse once a year—or no matter how often—for it will simply not be reviewed and will be killed by silence. . . . As I consider that Pound and Lewis are the only writers in London whose work is worth pushing, this worries me. I know that Pound's lack of tact has done him great harm. But I am worried as to what is to become of him.[1]

Quinn brought about Pound's appointment as Paris correspondent of the *Dial* which 'had a great effect in raising his spirits', Eliot reported on 10 May.

'I am gradually putting a prose book together—I think much more solid than the first attempt; and there is a possibility of getting a good publisher to take it here. But London "good publishers" are very cautious.'[2] However, on 20 April, Methuen contracted for 'A Volume of Essays'; by 27 July Eliot was, he told his mother, 'in the midst of my final activities, which are beginning to look like a book', and to his 'great relief' *The Sacred Wood* was ready for posting on 9 August. Shortly afterwards he left with Wyndham Lewis for a holiday in France which led to their first meeting with James Joyce.[3] On his return he resumed his search for a new flat and was absorbed in negotiations when the proof arrived. As it had to be checked 'very rapidly' to be in time for autumn publication, he 'got Pound and his wife also to help in correcting it, but even so it entailed a lot of work, what with all the quotations in various languages which had to be verified and were found to have lots of mistakes in them'.[4]

Overwrought by the problems of finding somewhere to live, Eliot longed for 'a

[1] 25 January.

[2] To Quinn, 26 March.

[3] See Wyndham Lewis's brilliant description in *Blasting & Bombardiering* (1937), pp. 270–6. For Eliot's account of Lewis's cycling mishaps on the same holiday (wrongly ascribed to 1921) see the *Hudson Review*, x. 2 (Summer 1957), [167]–170.

[4] To his Mother, 20 September.

period of tranquility to do a poem that I have in mind'.[1] He and Vivien had come to loathe their neighbourhood 'on account of the noise and sordidness',[2] and 'I simply cannot any longer work where we are or ever rest'.[3] When at last they found a suitable flat he wrote to his mother on 6 October: 'Everything is so expensive, so fearfully expensive, that it is bound to cripple one and prevent one from being able to do other things —and it means counting very close at that; and then one is so anxious lest it prove to have some unexpected drawback when one finally gets into it. We have been worried out of our wits.'

Another strain was the sudden, dangerous illness of Vivien's father, who underwent two operations. She collapsed when the tension eased.

'I am rather tired of [*The Sacred Wood*] now, as I am so anxious to get on to new work, and I should more enjoy being praised if I were engaged on something which I thought better or more important. I think I shall be able to do so, soon.'[4]

1921 You appear, like me, to lead a very exhausting life, with the leisure that you want always a mirage ahead of you, your holidays always disturbed by unforeseen (or foreseen) calamities [Eliot told Quinn]. But, of course your work is far more difficult and worrying than mine. Even what I do —I am dealing alone with all the debts and claims of the bank under the various Peace Treaties —sometimes takes a good deal of thought and strength. When my private life is uneventful, that is not serious enough to matter, but when I have private anxieties on my mind it is too much. Now I am expecting my mother from Boston in a few weeks. As she is 77, and not so strong as she was when I saw her last, that will be another anxiety as well as a joy.

I have not yet had any practical reason to regret my livelihood, in the circumstances. Had I joined the *Athenaeum* two years ago, I should now be desperate, as the *Athenaeum* has disappeared, and I am certain that I, at least, would not have been one of those to find a safe nest in the *Nation*. The chief drawback to my present mode of life is the lack of *continuous* time, not getting more than a few hours together for myself, which breaks the concentration required for turning out a poem of any length.

Eliot wished he could have followed Pound as the London agent of the *Dial*, 'but I have been quite incapacitated this winter, and I never did get about or pick up as many people as he did'.

Did I tell you that I met Joyce in Paris last autumn? I found him quite charming, and liked him; though I can see that he is certainly a handful, with the true fanatic's conviction that everyone ought to forward the interests of his work. It is, however, the conviction of the fanatic, and not the artfulness or pertinacity of ordinary push; and the latter part of *Ulysses*, which I have been reading in manuscript, is truly magnificent.

The Sacred Wood 'is a very imperfect production, and there are only four or five of the papers which I should like to save for a definitive book. I have no idea whether it has sold either here or in America. The reviews have been various.' He was not anxious

1 To his Mother, 20 September.
2 Idem, 3 July.
3 Idem, 6 October.
4 Idem, 2 December.

to produce another book of essays for a year or two and meanwhile he was 'wishful to finish a long poem' (as he still described *The Waste Land*) which was now 'partly on paper'.[1]

Writing to Richard Aldington on 16 August, Eliot made an allusion to the advent of the *Criterion*:

What I must explain at this point is, *in strict confidence*, that there is a possibility of a new literary venture, to be financed up to a certain (too certain) point, in which, (if it comes off) I shall be deeply involved. This should soon be decided, and I shall then want to discuss it with you at length. But if it is realised, I shall probably have little time for outside writing. It will not yield me much beyond the price of my own contributions, if that, but it might be interesting.

The Eliots moved to Wigmore Street for the summer so that his mother and sister, Marian, could occupy their flat in Clarence Gate Gardens. Henry came too for part of the visit. 'These new and yet old relationships involve immense tact and innumerable adjustments. One sees lots of things one never saw before etc.'[2] Despite her son's fears, Mrs. Eliot proved 'terrifyingly energetic' for her age. Vivien stayed in town at first, but as she was under medical orders to be in the country at that time of year, Eliot insisted on her getting away whenever possible.

Eliot's own health was deteriorating, and in late September Vivien arranged for him to see a specialist.

I have had much to do, and have felt so ill that it has taken me twice as long to do it. I have seen the specialist (said to be the best in London) who made his tests, and said that I must go away *at once* for three months quite alone, and away from anyone, not exert my mind at all, and follow his strict rules for every hour of the day. So I have been given leave by the bank for that period, very generously—they continue to pay my salary. I am going in about a week, as soon as I have taught enough knowledge of my work to a substitute. I did not anticipate such a medical verdict, and the prospect does not fill me with anything but dread. . . .

Perhaps you will think: why not simply chuck the bank, rest, and begin journalism. But I simply feel too ill for that, and I am sure that this would be the worst possible moment for such a change. I should have to brace myself to a new effort, instead of relaxing, and I should worry myself in a short time into a far worse state. So I am sure you will agree with me that the best thing is to follow the doctor's orders for the three months and not make any plans beyond that date. . . . I really feel very shaky, and seem to have gone down rapidly since my family left.[3]

I am going to Margate tomorrow, and expect to stay at least a month. I am supposed to be alone, but I could not bear the idea of starting this treatment quite alone in a strange place, and I have asked my wife to come with me and stay with me as long as she is willing. . . . After that I purpose to go abroad, probably to a small cottage with a verandah which Lady Rothermere has offered me, in the mountains back of Monte Carlo (La Tourbie). I want Vivien to cross with me and go somewhere healthy. If she does, would you be able to house a small cat which we are very fond of? . . . It is a very good mouser.[4]

1 9 May.
2 To Richard Aldington, 23 June.
3 Idem, undated, possibly 3 October.
4 Idem, undated, possibly 11 October.

From Margate he appealed to Julian Huxley for advice a fortnight later:

> I went to this specialist on account of his great name, which I knew would bear weight with my employers. But since I have been here I have wondered whether he is quite the best man for me as he is known as a nerve man and I want rather a specialist in psychological troubles. Ottoline Morrell has strongly advised me to go to [Dr. Roger] Vittoz in Lausanne and incidentally mentioned that you had been to him. This is all that I know about him. There are so few good specialists in this line that one wants to have more precise testimony of a man's value before trying him—especially as I cannot afford to go to Switzerland which is so expensive, unless the benefit is likely to justify the expense. . . . If you recommend him, perhaps you know also of some moderate priced pension or hotel.[1]

On the 31st Eliot thanked Huxley 'very much indeed for [his] full and satisfactory letter. I shall go to Vittoz. . . . He sounds just the man I want. I am glad you confirm my opinion of English doctors. They seem to specialise either in nerves or insanity!'

Telling Aldington of his change of plan, Eliot noted, 'I am satisfied, since being here, that my "nerves" are a very mild affair, due not to overwork but to an aboulie and emotional derangement which has been a lifelong affliction. Nothing wrong with my mind—.'[2]

He left Margate on 12 November, and after a week at home, set out on the 18th for Lausanne, leaving Vivien in Paris *en route*.

> The great thing I am trying to learn [he wrote from Switzerland] is how to use all my energy without waste, to be *calm* when there is nothing to be gained by worry, and to concentrate without effort. I hope that I shall place less strain upon Vivien who has had to do so much *thinking* for me . . . I am very much better, and not miserable here—at least there are people of many nationalities, which I always like. . . . I am certainly well enough to be working on a poem![3]

1922 Early in January Eliot returned to London, after spending a few days in Paris, where he submitted the manuscript of *The Waste Land* to Pound's maieutic skill.

'Eliot came back from his Lausanne specialist looking OK; and with a damn good poem (19 pages) in his suitcase; same finished up here; and shd be out in Dial soon, if Thayer isn't utterly nutty.

'About enough, Eliot's poem, to make the rest of us shut up shop', Pound remarked to Quinn on 21 February, adding characteristically: 'I haven't done so. . . .'

> I have written, mostly when I was at Lausanne for treatment last winter, a long poem of about 450 words [lines], which, with notes I am adding, will make a book of 30 to 40 pages [Eliot told Quinn on 25 June]. I think it is the best I have ever done, and Pound thinks so too. Pound introduced me to Liveright in Paris, and Liveright made me the offer of 15% royalty and $150 in advance. I thought I ought to give Knopf the option, and did so; but Knopf said that it was too late for his autumn list this year, and Liveright offered to publish it this autumn, so I cabled to him to say he could have it.

[1] 26 October. [2] 6 November. [3] To Henry Eliot, 13 December.

When the contract came, Eliot thought it 'extremely vague . . . and tantamount to selling . . . the book outright for $150'. Asking Quinn to prepare a contract similar to the one he made with Knopf for the *Poems*, he added: 'I am sending you as quickly as possible a copy of the poem merely for your own interest, and I shall send you later the complete typescript with the notes, in the form to be handed to the publisher.' On 19 July Eliot resumed:

. . . I have yesterday a mild letter from Liveright which sounds as if he would come to terms. As it is now so late I am enclosing the typescript to hand to him when the contract is complete, or to hold if he does not complete. I had wished to type it out fair, but I did not wish to delay it any longer. This will do for him to get on with, and I shall rush forward the notes to go at the end. I only hope the printers are not allowed to bitch the punctuation and the spacing, as that is very important for the sense. . . . I should like to present you the MSS of the Waste Land, if you would care to have it—when I say MSS, I mean that it is partly MSS and partly typescript, with Ezra's and my alterations scrawled all over it.

Quinn replied with a fourteen-page letter extending from 28 July to 1 August. Liveright had signed the fresh contract 'without the change of a word'. Eliot had not given him the title of the book, but fortunately Pound had put it in a postscript.

Waste Land is one of the best things you have done, though I imagine that Liveright may be a little disappointed [with the size], but I think he will go through with it. It is for the elect or the remnant or the select few or the superior guys, or any word that you may choose, for the small numbers of readers that it is certain to have. I shall be glad to have the MS. of *Waste Land* but I shan't let you 'present it to me'. When you finish the whole thing, poetry and prose, if you will send the MS. or the MSS. to me, I shall be glad to have it, but you must agree to the condition that I send you a draft for what I think it is worth. I shall feel happier to do it that way.

Eliot was firm:

I certainly cannot accept your proposal to purchase the manuscript at your own price, and if you will not accept it in recognition of what you have done for me lately and in the past, it will not be any pleasure to me to sell it to you. I therefore hope that you will accept it. But as I feel that perhaps you like some of my early poems best I should be glad, for example, to send you the manuscript of Prufrocks [*sic*] instead, and I hope you will let me do this.[1]

The contract seemed to him 'as perfect as it is possible for a contract to be'. He enclosed a circular about the *Criterion* 'for your amusement. One never knows whether any public activity of this sort is worth while but it is interesting to make such an attempt at least once in one's life; if it succeeds—as far as anything of the sort can be expected to succeed—it will be of satisfaction to me; meanwhile it is a kind of experience.'[2]

While completing *The Waste Land* in January Eliot had written to Scofield Thayer to ask what the *Dial* would offer for it, and the answer, $150, sight unseen, did not displease him. But his thoughts were already turning to book publication when he and

[1] 21 August. [2] Ibid. Quinn took out three subscriptions.

Pound heard that the magazine had paid George Moore a hundred pounds for his short story, *Peronnik the Fool*; they were so incensed that Eliot cabled Thayer that he could not accept less than £856. The matter did not end there. Eliot recounted to Quinn: 'A few days ago I had an attractive proposal from Mr. Watson of the *Dial* who are very anxious to publish the poem. . . . They suggested getting Liveright to postpone the date of publication as a book, but I have written to them to say that it seemed to me too late to be proper to make any change now and that I should not care to trouble either Mr. Liveright or particularly yourself with any questions of alterations in the contract.'[1] Nevertheless Gilbert Seldes, the Managing Editor of the *Dial*, approached Quinn and Liveright. They met in Quinn's office on 7 September and soon came to an agreement: Eliot would receive the annual *Dial* award of $2,000, the *Dial* would publish the poem without notes and buy 350 copies of the book; in return, Liveright would allow them prior publication.[2]

'So everything is all right', Quinn wrote to Eliot after the meeting. 'It was a pleasure to do this little job for you today.'

> We won't quarrel about the MS. of The Waste Land. I'll accept it from you, not 'for what I have lately done for you and in the past', but as a mark of friendship, but on this condition: That you will let me purchase of you the MS. of the Early Poems that you referred to. If you have the Prufrock only, then I'll purchase that. But if you have the MS. of the whole volume of your poems, including the Prufrock, I should *greatly value* that, and then I'll have two complete manuscripts of yours. If you leave to me the fixing of what the MS. of those poems would be worth, I would discuss the matter with one or two dealers in rare books and manuscripts and autograph letters and would be guided by their advice. If I had to choose between the MS. of The Waste Land and the Notes and the Prufrock MS. alone, I would choose The Waste Land MS. But I feel sure that you'll agree to my condition that I pay you for the MS. of the Early Poems. That meets your point and it gives me another MS. of yours, and each of us will be happy.

> I am quite overwhelmed by your letter, by all that you have done for me, by the results that you have effected, and by your endless kindness [Eliot replied on 21 September]. In fact, the greatest pleasure of all that it has given me is the thought that there should be anybody in the world who would take such an immense amount of pains on my behalf. The thought of this will be a permanent satisfaction to me.
>
> My only regret (which may seem in the circumstances either ungracious or hypocritical) is that this award should come to me before it has been given to Pound. I feel that he deserves the recognition much more than I do, certainly 'for his services to Letters', and I feel that I ought to have been made to wait until after he had received this public testimony. In the manuscript of *The Waste Land* which I am sending you, you will see the evidences of his work, and I think that this manuscript is worth preserving in its present form solely for the reason that it is the only evidence of the difference which his criticism has made to this poem. . . .

Disturbed to learn from Aldington that Eliot was 'going to pieces' again less than

[1] 21 August.

[2] *The Waste Land* was published 'almost simultaneously (*ca.* 15 October)' in the *Criterion* and the *Dial*. The first edition (with notes) appeared on 15 December.

three months after treatment in Lausanne, Pound from Paris revived on an international scale his earlier scheme to release Eliot from the bank. Known as *Bel Esprit*, it needed thirty guarantors of £10 a year for an indefinite period, and was presented vigorously to Pound's friends, and in the *New Age*. Quinn pledged $300 for five years. Eliot, who had not been consulted, found the situation 'embarrassing and fatiguing . . . in spite of the motives, which I appreciate. I think . . . that the method proposed by Ezra is rather bordering on the precarious and slightly undignified charity.'[1] The uncertainty of guarantees beyond the first year (for which £300 had been promised), combined with Eliot's lack of enthusiasm, put an end to a generous conception. Unhappily, the publicity caused Eliot to be

> harassed by two episodes, one a libellous remark in the [*Liverpool Daily Post and Mercury*][2] stating that I had been offered £800 two years ago to leave the bank, and that I accepted the money and declined to keep my promise; and the other an anonymous insulting letter offering me 6*d*. for the collection which the writer had heard was being taken up for me. I have had to pursue both these matters, and it has involved a great deal of consultation with friends [and] with legal advisers . . . [These attacks] have greatly impaired for the time being the good effects of the regime which [Vivien] has been pursuing. We are both completely worn out. It is as much the damage that these things have done in impairing the . . . months of dogged, and persistent efforts she has made, as anything else about the matter, that makes me angry. But of course I should in any case have had to take action about the libel as persistence of such reports might eventually cause a catastrophe to my position at the bank, and for this reason they could more easily ruin me than they might some people.[3]

> Vivien has been very tired since Christmas. She sat up to dinner in the evening on that day for the first time in months . . . she has been living since last July under the severest and most spartan regimen that I have ever known, which has been much more difficult than any regimen in a nursing home or sanatorium because, living it in the midst of ordinary life imposes much more responsibility on her and requires infinite tenacity of purpose; she has not been able to deviate in the slightest from the most limited and particular diet, and she has not been able to take ordinary exercise, only the special exercises prescribed for her and she has hardly seen anybody. I have never known anybody stick to a thing with such persistence and courage, often with relapses which made her feel that the whole thing was useless. She has certainly made great gains by it, but I think that the strain of such a mode of life is beginning to tell on her, and lately she has been sleeping very badly indeed. If I were not tied to the bank I could have gone abroad with her for a time; as it is she is not only under the strain of her own treatment but the strain of our very tense and always rushed and overworked mode of life.[4]

'As for *The Waste Land*, that is a thing of the past so far as I am concerned and I am now feeling toward a new form and style.'[5]

[1] To Richard Aldington, 30 June.
[2] 16 November.
[3] To Henry Eliot, 8 December.
[4] To Henry Eliot, 31 December.
[5] To Richard Aldington, 15 November.

1923 Quinn received the manuscripts in mid-January, but owing to ill health and overwork he was unable to acknowledge them until 26 February. He had read the full text of *The Waste Land* 'with great interest' and 'noted the evidence of Pound's criticism on the poem. Personally I should not have cut out some of the parts that Pound advised you to cut out.' He would hold the material 'largely in trust' for Eliot who could have copies of any part of it whenever he wished. Accepting *The Waste Land* as a gift he had had the poems valued:

> With the notebook and loose sheets of paper . . . there are some fifty-three pages of manuscript in the book and some five or six pages of loose manuscript, making roughly sixty pages. Then there are the typewritten drafts, which Drake [a book dealer] did not rank as manuscript and disregarded in his valuation. He thought that a payment of about $2 a page, which would be about $120, would be 'about right'. But I thought his figures were somewhat conservative and I am sending you London draft to your order for £29.14.10, the equivalent at the present rate of exchange of $140, which I think is fair and reasonable I trust you will agree with me. In fixing this price I am taking into consideration the condition stated in your letter, namely, that I 'pay the present fair value of it, disregarding any prospective or future value'.

Now that the second impression of *The Waste Land* was selling well Quinn revealed 'confidentially, the success of the book was rather a surprise to Liveright. He almost had cold feet about it before the *Dial* suggestion was made.'

Eliot answered on 12 March: 'I consider your payment for the manuscript very generous indeed, and feel that you have thwarted me in my attempt to repay you in some way for all that you have done.'

After mentioning that he had not yet received the $150 Liveright promised on publication, he unburdened himself:

> I am now in the midst of a terrific crisis. I wish to heaven that I had never taken up the *Criterion*. It seemed a good thing, and it is a good thing, but although it is a pity to drop such a promising beginning I may very soon have to drop it and I am quite sincere when I wish that I had never undertaken it. It has been an evergrowing responsibility . . . a great *expense* to me and I have not got a penny out of it: there is not enough money to run it and pay me too. I hoped that it would be a solid thing for me, but there is no longer *time* to wait for that. I think the work and worry have taken 10 years off my life. I have sunk the whole of my strength for the past 18 months into this confounded paper, when I ought to have been minding my business and doing my own writing. The paper has therefore done me more harm than good. The present situation is this: that I must either give up the bank at once and find some work which would take less of my time—thereby sacrificing part of an income every penny of which I need—or else I must give up the *Criterion* before my health crashes and I am no longer able to perform my bank work. I am now offered the post of literary editor of the *Nation*, at £200 a year less than my present salary and with no assurance that the job will last longer than six months, and if I take that I shall have to go straight into new work, which for the first six months will be very difficult and worrying, at a moment when I feel much more like going into a sanatorium. In order to carry on the *Criterion* I have had to neglect not only the writing I ought to be doing but my private affairs of every description which for some time past I have not had a moment to deal with. I have not even time

to go to a dentist or to have my hair cut, and at the same time I see the *Criterion* full of most glaring defects which I could only avoid by having still more time for it to devour, and at the same time I am simply unfit to take risks which in any case I should not be justified in taking.

In ink was written 'I am worn out, I cannot go on'.

Quinn cabled:[1] 'If you decide accept offer post literary editor *Nation* you may count upon six hundred dollars annually for five years four hundred from me and two hundred from Otto Kahn. But think that *Nation* should give you contract providing for one year's pay in case termination.' Having ascertained that the belated $150 had been sent on 15 March, he disclosed in a fatherly letter that, prompted by the *Bel Esprit* scheme, he had sent Eliot's books to certain people with the suggestion that they might care to guarantee a regular sum for five years, but so far only Otto Kahn, the international banker, had responded. Quinn would have liked to double his own contribution but he was already heavily committed to helping Sir Horace Plunkett to re-establish the *Irish Statesman*. Nevertheless he was hopeful that he might be able to raise at least $1,000.

'*Nation* off failing guarantee', Eliot apprised him on 2 April. 'Also unable wait necessary notice bank. Does extraordinarily generous offer hold if bad health forces leave bank without alternative position. Thank Kahn. Await letter.'

Quinn replied: 'Offer holds for five years unconditional.'

It was not until 26 April that Eliot wrote

from a small cottage near Chichester, which I took for a year because it was essential that my wife should be in the country. I took my 3 weeks annual holiday in order to get her started here. Unfortunately, she had a very bad colitis attack just before we came, and has been ill here—under most uncomfortable conditions—ever since; having the specialist from London twice a week, and the local man twice a day, and her mother most of the time. Another man is coming from London on Saturday. They have called it septic influenza and then thought it was turning to pneumonia, and have been taking analyses. Meanwhile she has wasted away to a skeleton, and my holiday is gone, and I feel a good deal more ill than when it started, and I shall not get a day more for a year. . . . I feel pretty well knocked out; the shock of thinking seven or eight times over that my wife was at the point of death was enough in itself. . . .

The *Nation* did not want to give more than six months' guarantee, and they wanted me at once if at all. I pointed out that this might be all right for a man who was already in journalism, but that it is quite different for a man who has to give up a secure post. I don't know whether I have ever explained this to you, but the Bank is a secure job for life, with a pension at sixty, and a year's salary and a pension for my wife in the event of my death. The main point, in any question of leaving the bank is (as I explained to Pound) the security for my wife. She will never be strong enough to shift for herself or to endure great privation. She will inherit very little, and not in the ordinary course for many years, and I must make reasonable provision for her before undertaking any adventures. I must explain also that owing to the terms of my father's will, any property coming to me is in trust, and reverts to the family on my death—instead of

[1] 27 March.

being left outright as to my brother and sisters. Thus my wife can get no benefit from my inheritance in the event of my death. My father disapproved of my residence in England.

I have gone into these details, for the first time, because it might appear, and I daresay has appeared to people who do not know my circumstances, that I am either very cowardly or very grasping. . . .

I do regard it as a disaster that I could not come to an arrangement with the *Nation*, and if the same post, or any similar post, should be open to me in the future, I should take it. I *mean* to leave the bank, and I *must* leave the bank, but I cannot say how soon or in what way.

I am at present trying to lay a foundation by investing every penny I can save. This is a very slow process, with the expenses which I have—the cost of the last fortnight, with the specialist down twice a week from London, local doctor twice daily, etc., etc., has been almost ruinous, and I shall not be able to put by any more for a long time to come.

In your letter you said that you would 'send me a cheque as soon as I acknowledged receipt of your letter'. . . . *But if you assumed that I was leaving the bank at once in any case*, and meant the money to be payable on my leaving the bank only, then I should like to know whether the guarantee of this $600 per annum for five years holds good whether I leave the bank to go into another job, such as an editorship, or whether my health forces me to leave without any job at all.

Otto Kahn's offer proved to be conditional on Eliot leaving the bank, but Quinn was 'perfectly willing to make his contribution unconditional, beginning now', and with his letter of 23 July he enclosed a draft for £86. 19*s.* 1*d.*, the equivalent of $400. 'You can count upon the second $400 in June 1924, and $400 in June 1925, in June 1926, and in June 1927. You can add this to the trust fund that you referred to or you can use it just as you please.'

For the moment Eliot was engaged 'in rather more tolerable work at the bank', editing 'a daily sheet of Extracts (commercial and financial) from the foreign press'. He had to be an authority on affairs in France, Italy, Spain, Rumania, Greece, Turkey and the U.S.A., and write a monthly article on foreign exchange.

I shall, of course, consider the money you sent as a trust, contingent upon my leaving the bank, and not dip into it unless in absolute need. I have been fairly near it, for my expenses in connection with my wife's illness have been terrific, running a country cottage as well as this flat, doctors' bills, medicines, fares, motor car rides, and always feeding at least one extra person as she must always have some relative or friend with her to do house-keeping, see to preparation of her special food etc. I wanted her to be under a German physician who seems just the man —he was here for a week, but she is not fit to go to Freiburg, even if things settle down, unless I can go with her and stay with her, and this I cannot do. I am not looking forward to the winter.

I have not attempted to express my thanks. It is really beyond words. But you have been a greater support and encouragement to me than I can possibly say. It is unique.[1]

1924 On 28 July John Quinn died at the age of fifty-four.

Eliot had paid his tribute in a letter written on 26 April 1923. Its practical spirit must have pleased the recipient:

. . . I have said nothing so far to show an atom of my appreciation of your extraordinary

[1] 4 October.

generosity and kindness. When I think of all you have done for me for years past in other ways, I do not know what more to say to convince you of the strength of my recognition. Perhaps I can only say that it is the greatest stimulus to me to commence the work I have in mind, which is more ambitious than anything I have ever done yet. And a stimulus to do my part to bring about the conditions which will make this work possible.

ABOUT THE MANUSCRIPTS

The packet containing the manuscripts was sent to Quinn by registered post on 23 October 1922, and reached his office at 31 Nassau Street, New York, on 13 January 1923.

They were not mentioned in Quinn's will, but formed part of the estate inherited by his sister, Julia (Mrs. William Anderson). After Mrs. Anderson's death in 1934, her widower and daughter, Mary (Mrs. Thomas F. Conroy) moved to a smaller apartment, and many cases of Quinn's papers were put in storage. It was not until the early 1950s, after a prolonged search, that Mrs. Conroy found the manuscripts.[1]

On 4 April 1958 she sold them to the Berg Collection of the New York Public Library for $18,000. The purchase remained private, neither Eliot nor Pound being told about it. The Curator, the late Dr. John D. Gordan, asked a common friend if she could arrange an appointment for him with Eliot to discuss 'a business matter' when he visited London in May that year. Eliot was in America at the time unfortunately, and Dr. Gordan made no further attempt to communicate with him.

I was informed of the acquisitions when Mr. James W. Henderson[2] gave me a microfilm of them, in the summer of 1968, with the request to observe secrecy until the Library issued a public statement on 25 October, the date of the publication of Professor B. L. Reid's biography, *The Man from New York: John Quinn and His Friends*.

Mrs. Conroy has presented the twenty-two letters and six cables from Eliot to her uncle to the Manuscript Division of the Library.

[1] Information in a letter from Mrs. Conroy to the Editor, 23 February 1970.

[2] Chief of the Research Libraries of the New York Public Library.

THE WASTE LAND

The manuscript-typescript of *The Waste Land* consists of fifty-four leaves (of which forty-seven are single), together with three receipted bills for the period 22 October to 12 November 1921, from The Albemarle Hotel, Cliftonville, Margate (where Eliot began his convalescence), and the label from the packet. There are no notes. Someone, possibly Eliot, has divided the leaves into two sections: the main text, and the miscellaneous poems which were considered for it; these now[1] contain forty-two leaves and twelve leaves respectively. An assortment of paper has been used.

V. E.

[1] When Dr. Donald Gallup was preparing his article on 'The "Lost" Manuscripts of T. S. Eliot' [*The Times Literary Supplement*, 3480 (7 November 1968), 1238–40], he transferred the drafts of 'From which a Venus Anadyomene', 'O City, City' (with 'London . . .' on the same page), 'The River Sweats', and 'Highbury bore me' from the second to the first section.

ACKNOWLEDGEMENTS

It is a pleasure to thank Mr. Ezra Pound, 'a wondrous necessary man' to my husband, for his hospitality and helpfulness. I am also obliged to him and Mrs. Pound for permission to use copyright material.

I owe a special debt to Dr. Lola L. Szladits, Curator of the Berg Collection of the New York Public Library, and to Dr. Donald Gallup of Yale University.

I wish to express my gratitude to Mr. James H. Henderson of the New York Public Library; to Mr. Robert W. Hill, Keeper of Manuscripts; to Mr. Harvey Simmonds, formerly of the Berg Collection; to Mrs. Thomas F. Conroy for permission to quote from the letters of John Quinn, and for private information; and to Mrs. Jeanne Robert Foster.

For help in various ways, I am very grateful to Dr. W. H. Bond, Mr. R. W. Burchfield and the staff of the Oxford English Dictionary Supplement, Dr. Joseph Chiari, Mr. Peter du Sautoy, Dame Helen Gardner, Mr. Robert Giroux, Mr. William Jovanovich, Professor G. Wilson Knight, Miss Mary Lascelles, Miss Hope Mirrlees, The Reverend Francis Sweeney, S.J., and Professor R. C. Zaehner.

No acknowledgements would be complete without mentioning my appreciation of the skill and care of the staff of the University Press, Oxford.

EDITORIAL POLICY

THE purpose of my Introduction is two-fold: to show the important part which John Quinn played in Eliot's life, and to enhance the reader's understanding of the poem by using Eliot's own words to describe some of the events and emotions of the years leading up to *The Waste Land*.

In preparing a transcript I have silently corrected obvious typing errors, and where a word intended for deletion has been imperfectly deleted, I have deleted it in full. Inaccurate spellings and quotations have been emended, in my footnotes, to the text of the first edition. In my Notes I have borne in mind that what may be apparent to an English reader might be obscure to an American one, and vice versa. It has been difficult to decide who cancelled certain lines, especially when both Eliot and Pound have worked on them together. Pound's annotations are printed in red, and Vivien Eliot's contributions are in italics with a cancelled broken line.

'Various critics have done me the honour to interpret the poem in terms of criticism of the contemporary world, have considered it, indeed, as an important bit of social criticism. To me it was only the relief of a personal and wholly insignificant grouse against life; it is just a piece of rhythmical grumbling.'

T. S. E.

Quoted by the late Professor Theodore Spencer during a lecture at Harvard University, and recorded by the late Henry Ware Eliot, Jr., the poet's brother.

THE WASTE LAND.

By

T.S.Eliot.

"Did he live his life again in every detail of desire, temptation, and surrender during that supreme moment of complete knowledge? He cried in a whisper at some image, at some vision, - he cried out twice, a cry that was no more than a breath -

'The horror! the Horror!'"

CONRAD.

THE WASTE LAND.

By

T. S. Eliot.

"Did he live his life again in every detail of desire, temptation, and surrender during that supreme moment of complete knowledge? He cried in a whisper at some image, at some vision,—he cried out twice, a cry that was no more than a breath—

'The horror! the horror!'"

CONRAD. (1)

HE DO THE POLICE IN DIFFERENT VOICES: Part I.

THE BURIAL OF THE DEAD.

First we had a couple of feelers down at Tom's place,
There was old Tom, boiled to the eyes, blind,
(Don't you remember that time after a dance,
Top hats and all, we and Silk Hat Harry,
And old Tom took us behind, brought out a bottle of fizz,
With old Jane, Tom's wife; and we got Joe to sing
"I'm proud of all the Irish blood that's in me,
"There's not a man can say a word agin me").
Then we had dinner in good form, and a couple of Bengal lights.
When we got into the show, up in Row A,
I tried to put my foot in the drum, and didn't the girl squeal,
She never did take to me, a nice guy- but rough;
The next thing we were out in the street, Oh was it cold!
When will you be good? Blew in to the Opera Exchange,
Sopped up some gin, sat in to the cork game,
Mr.Fay was there, singing "The Maid of the Mill";
Then we thought we'd breeze along and take a walk.
Then we lost Steve.
("I turned up an hour later down at Myrtle's place.
What d'y' mean, she says, at two o'clock in the morning,
I'm not in business here for guys like you;
We've only had a raid last week, I've been warned twice.
~~Sergeant, I said~~, I've kept a decent house for twenty years,
There's three gents from the Buckingham Club upstairs now,
I'm going to retire and live on a farm, she says,
There's no money in it now, what with the damage done,
And the reputation the place gets, ~~on account~~ of a few bar-flies,
I've kept a clean house for twenty years, she says,
And the gents from the Buckingham Club know they're safe here;
You was well introduced, but this is the last of you.
Get me a woman, I said; you're too drunk, she said,
But she gave me a bed, and a bath, and ham and eggs,
And now you go get a shave, she said; ~~I had a good laugh~~,
Myrtle ~~was~~ always ~~a good sport~~.
We'd just gone up the alley, a fly cop came along,
Looking for trouble; committing a nuisance, he said,
You come on to the station. I'm sorry, I said,
It's no use being sorry, he said; let me get my hat, I said.
Well by a stroke of luck who came by but Mr.Donavan.
What's this,officer. You're new on this beat, aint you?
~~I thought so. You know who I am? Yes, I do,~~
~~Saidd the fresh cop, very peevish.~~ Then let it alone,
These gents are particular friends of mine.
-Wasn't it luck? Then we went to the German Club,
~~We~~ and Mr.Donavan and his friend ~~Joe Leahy~~,
~~Found it shut.~~ I want to get home, said the cabman,
We all go the same way home, said Mr.Donavan,
Cheer up, Trixie and Stella; and put his foot through the window.
The next I know the old cab was hauled up on the avenue,
And the cabman and little Ben Levin the tailor,
The one who read George Meredith,
Were running a hundred yards on a bet,
And Mr.Donavan holding the watch.
So I got out to see the sunrise, and walked home.

HE DO THE POLICE IN DIFFERENT VOICES (1): Part I.

THE BURIAL OF THE DEAD.

First we had a couple of feelers down at Tom's place,
There was old Tom, boiled to the eyes, blind,
(Don't you remember that time after a dance,
Top hats and all, we and Silk Hat Harry,
And old Tom took us behind, brought out a bottle of fizz,
With old Jane, Tom's wife; and we got Joe to sing ~~Meet me in the shadow of the watermelon Vine~~
"I'm proud of all the Irish blood that's in me,
"There's not a man can say a word agin me"). (2) ~~Eva Iva Uva Emmaline~~ (3)
Then we had dinner in good form, and a couple of Bengal lights. (4)
When we got into the show, up in Row A, Tease, Squeeze lovin & wooin
I tried to put my foot in the drum, and didn't the girl squeal, Say Kid what're y' doin' (5)
She never did take to me, a nice guy—but rough;
The next thing we were out in the street, Oh was it cold!
When will you be good? Blew in to the Opera Exchange, (6)
Sopped up some gin, sat in to the cork game,
Mr. Fay was there, singing "The Maid of the Mill"; (7)
Then we thought we'd breeze along and take a walk.
Then we lost Steve.
—("I turned up an hour later down at Myrtle's place.
What d'y' mean, she says, at two o'clock in the morning,
I'm not in business here for guys like you;
We've only had a raid last week, I've been warned twice.
~~Sergeant, I said~~, I've kept a decent house for twenty years, she says
There's three gents from the Buckingham Club upstairs now,
I'm going to retire and live on a farm, she says,
There's no money in it now, what with the damage done,
And the reputation the place gets, ~~on account~~ off of a few bar-flies,
I've kept a clean house for twenty years, she says,
And the gents from the Buckingham Club know they're safe here;
You was well introduced, but this is the last of you.
Get me a woman, I said; you're too drunk, she said,
But she gave me a bed, and a bath, and ham and eggs,
And now you go get a shave, she said; ~~I had a good laugh~~, ~~couple of laughs (?)~~
Myrtle ~~was~~ always ~~a good sport").~~ treated me white. ~~real~~
—We'd just gone up the alley, a fly cop came along, ~~good (?)~~ ~~good laugh~~
Looking for trouble; committing a nuisance, he said,
You come on to the station. I'm sorry, I said,
It's no use being sorry, he said; let me get my hat, I said.
Well by a stroke of luck who came by but Mr. Donavan.
What's this, officer. You're new on this beat, aint you?
~~I thought so. You know who I am? Yes, I do,~~ ~~me~~?
~~Said the fresh cop, very peevish.~~ Then let it alone,
These gents are particular friends of mine.
—Wasn't it luck? Then we went to the German Club, Gus (8)
Us ~~We~~ and Mr. Donavan and his friend ~~Joe Leahy,~~ ~~Heinie~~ Krutzsch
F~~ound it shut.~~ I want to get home, said the cabman,
We all go the same way home, said Mr. Donavan,
Cheer up, Trixie and Stella; and put his foot through the window.
The next I know the old cab was hauled up on the avenue,
And the cabman and little Ben Levin the tailor,
The one who read George Meredith, (9)
Were running a hundred yards on a bet,
And Mr. Donavan holding the watch.
So I got out to see the sunrise, and walked home.

Typescript revised in pencil and in ink. Eliot has cancelled the page lightly in pencil. Unpublished.

* * * *

April is the cruellest month, breeding
Lilacs out of the dead land, mixing
Memory and desire, stirring
Dull roots with spring rain.
Winter kept us warm, covering
Earth in forgetful snow, feeding
A little life with dried tubers.
Summer surprised us, coming over the Königssee
With a shower of rain; we stopped in the colonnade,
And went on in sunlight, into the Hofgarten,
And drank coffee, talking an hour.
Bin gar keine Russin, stamm' aus Litauen, echt deutsch.
And when we were children, staying at the archduke's,
My cousin's, he took me out on a sled,
And I was frightened. He said, Marie,
Marie, hold on tight. And down we went.
In the mountains, there you feel free.
I read, much of the night, and go south in the winter.

* * * *

What are the roots that clutch, what branches grew
Out of this stony rubbish? Son of man,
You cannot say, or guess, for you know only
A heap of broken images, where the sun beats,
And the dead tree gives no shelter, the cricket no relief,
And the dry stone no sound of water. Only
There is shadow under this red rock,
(Come in under the shadow of this red rock),
~~And~~ I will show you something different from either
Your shadow at morning striding behind you
Or your shadow at evening rising to meet you;
I will show you fear in a handful of dust.

* * * *

~~Main~~ Frisch ~~schwebt~~ weht der Wind
Der Heimat zu,
Mein Irisch' Kind,
Wo weilest du?
"You gave me hyacinths first a year ago;
"They called me the hyacinth girl".
-Yet when we came back, late, from the hyacinth garden,
Your arms full, and your hair wet, I could not
Speak, and my eyes failed, I was neither
Living nor dead, and I knew nothing,
Looking into the heart of light, the silence.

Öd' und leer das Meer

Madame Sosostris, famous clairvoyante
Had a bad cold, nevertheless
Is known to be the wisest woman in Europe,
With a wicked pack of cards. Here, said she,
Is your card, the drowned Phoenician Sailor,
~~(Those are pearls that were his eyes. Look!)~~
Here is Belladonna, the Lady of the Rocks,
The lady of situations,

2.

* * * *

April is the cruellest month, breeding
Lilacs out of the dead land, mixing
Memory and desire, stirring
Dull roots with spring rain.
Winter kept us warm, covering
Earth in forgetful snow, feeding
A little life with dried tubers.
Summer surprised us, coming over the Königssee
With a shower of rain; we stopped in the colonnade,
And went on in sunlight, into the Hofgarten,
And drank coffee, talking an hour.
Bin gar keine Russin, stamm' aus Litauen, echt deutsch.
And when we were children, staying at the archduke's, (1)
My cousin's, he took me out on a sled,
And I was frightened. He said, Marie,
Marie, hold on tight. And down we went.
In the mountains, there you feel free.
I read, much of the night, and go south in the winter.

* * * *

What are the roots that clutch, what branches grow
Out of this stony rubbish? Son of man,
You cannot say, or guess, for you know only
A heap of broken images, where the sun beats,
And the dead tree gives no shelter, the cricket no relief,
And the dry stone no sound of water. Only
There is shadow under this red rock,
(Come in under the shadow of this red rock),
~~And~~ I will show you something different from either
Your shadow at morning striding behind you
Or your shadow at evening rising to meet you;
I will show you fear in a handful of dust.

* * * *

weht
~~Mein~~ Frisch ~~schwebt~~ der Wind
Der Heimat zu,
Mein Irisch' Kind,
Wo weilest du?
"You gave me hyacinths first a year ago; ?
"They called me the hyacinth girl". Marianne (2)
—Yet when we came back, late, from the hyacinth garden,
Your arms full, and your hair wet, I could not
Speak, and my eyes failed, I was neither
Living nor dead, and I knew nothing,
Looking into the heart of light, the silence.
Öd' und leer das Meer.

Madame Sosostris, famous clairvoyante
Had a bad cold, nevertheless
Is known to be the wisest woman in Europe,
With a wicked pack of cards. Here, said she,
Is your card, the drowned Phoenician Sailor,
~~(Those are pearls that were his eyes. Look!)~~
Here is Belladonna, the Lady of the Rocks,
The lady of situations,

Typescript on two leaves, of lines 1–76. Revised in pencil and in ink, with Pound's marginalia in pencil.

Here is the man with three staves, and here the Wheel,
And here is the one-eyed merchant, and this card,
Which is blank, is something he carries on his back,
Which I am forbidden to see. I look in vain
For the Hanged Man. Fear death by water.
I see crowds of people, walking round in a ring.
~~(I John saw these things, and heard them).~~
Thank you. If you see dear Mrs. Equitone,
Tell her I bring the horoscope myself,
One must be so careful these days.

Unreal
~~Terrible~~ City, I have sometimes seen and see
Under the brown fog of your winter dawn
A crowd flow over London Bridge, so many,
I had not thought death had undone so many.
Sighs, short and infrequent, were ~~expired~~,
And each ~~one~~ ~~kept~~ his eyes before his feet.
Flowed up the hill and down King William Street,
~~To where Saint Mary Woolnoth kept the time,~~
~~With a dead sound on the final stroke of nine.~~
There I saw one I knew, and stopped him, crying: "Stetson!
"You who were with me in the ships at Mylae!
"That corpse you planted last year in your garden,
"Has it begun to sprout? Will it bloom this year?"
"Or has the sudden frost disturbed its bed?
"Oh keep the Dog far hence, that's ~~foe~~ to men,
"Or with his nails he'll dig it up again!
"You! hypocrite lecteur,- mon semblable,- mon frere!"

fisher King
~~King fishing~~

Here is the man with three staves, and here the Wheel,
And here is the one-eyed merchant, and this card,
Which is blank, is something he carries on his back,
Which I am forbidden to see. I look in vain
For the Hanged Man. Fear death by water.
I see crowds of people, walking round in a ring.
~~(I John saw these things, and heard them)~~. (1)
Thank you. If you see dear Mrs. Equitone,
Tell her I bring the horoscope myself,
One must be so careful these days.

Unreal
~~Terrible~~ City, I have sometimes seen and see
Under the brown fog of your winter dawn
A crowd flow over London Bridge, so many,
I had not thought death had undone so many.
~~held~~ Sighs, short and infrequent, were ~~expired~~, ~~exhaled~~. ~~expired~~. exhaled. J. J. (2)
fixed And each ~~one~~ ~~kept~~ his eyes before his feet.
Flowed up the hill and down King William Street, Blake. (3)
man ~~To where Saint Mary Woolnoth kept the time,~~ Too
~~With a dead sound on the final stroke of nine.~~ ~~old~~/often
There I saw one I knew, and stopped him, crying: "Stetson! used
"You who were with me in the ships at Mylae!
"That corpse you planted last year in your garden,
"Has it begun to sprout? Will it bloom this year?"
"Or has the sudden frost disturbed its bed?
"Oh keep the Dog far hence, that's ~~foe~~ to men, /friend
"Or with his nails he'll dig it up again!
"You! hypocrite lecteur,—mon semblable,—mon frère!"

yet?

HE DO THE POLICE IN DIFFERENT VOICES: Part II.

A Game of Chess.

~~IN THE CAGE.~~

The Chair she sat in, like a burnished throne
Glowed on the marble, where the swinging glass
Held up by standards wrought with golden vines
From which one tender Cupidon peeped out
(Another hid his eyes behind his wing)
Doubled the flames of seven-branched candelabra
Reflecting light upon the table ~~whaxa~~ as
The glitter of her jewels rose to meet ~~ixx~~ it,
From satin cases poured in rich profusion;
In vials of ivory and coloured glass
Unstoppered, lurked her strange synthetic perfumes
Unguent, powdered, or liquid- troubled, confused
And drowned the sense in odours; stirred by the air
That freshened from the window, these ascended,
Fattening the candle flames, ~~which were~~ prolonged,
~~And~~ flung their smoke into the laquenaria,
Stirring the pattern on the coffered ceiling.
Upon the hearth huge sea-wood fed with copper
Burned green and orange, framed by the coloured stone,
In which sad light a carved dolphin swam;
Above the antique mantel was displayed
In pigment, ~~but so lively, you had thought~~
A window gave upon the sylvan scene,
The change of Philomel, by the barbarous king
So rudely forced, yet ~~xtixk~~ there the nightingale
Filled all the desert with inviolable voice,
And still she cried (and still the world pursues)
Jug Jug, into ~~the~~ dirty ear ~~of death; lust,~~
~~And other tales, from the~~ old stumps and bloody ends of time
Were told upon the walls, ~~whose~~ staring forms
Leaned out, ~~and~~ hushed the room ~~and~~ closed it ~~in~~.
~~There~~ were footsteps on the stair,
Under the firelight, under the brush, her hair
Spread out in ~~little~~ fiery points ~~of will~~
Glowed into words, then would be savagely still.

"My nerves are bad tonight. Yes, bad. Stay with me.
"Speak to me. Why do you never speak. Speak.
"What are you thinking of? What thinking? ~~Thinkx~~ What?
"I never know what you are thinking. Think".

I think we met first in rats' alley,
Where the dead men lost their bones.

"What is that noise?"

The wind under the door.

"What is that noise now? What is the wind doing?"

HE DO THE POLICE IN DIFFERENT VOICES: Part II.

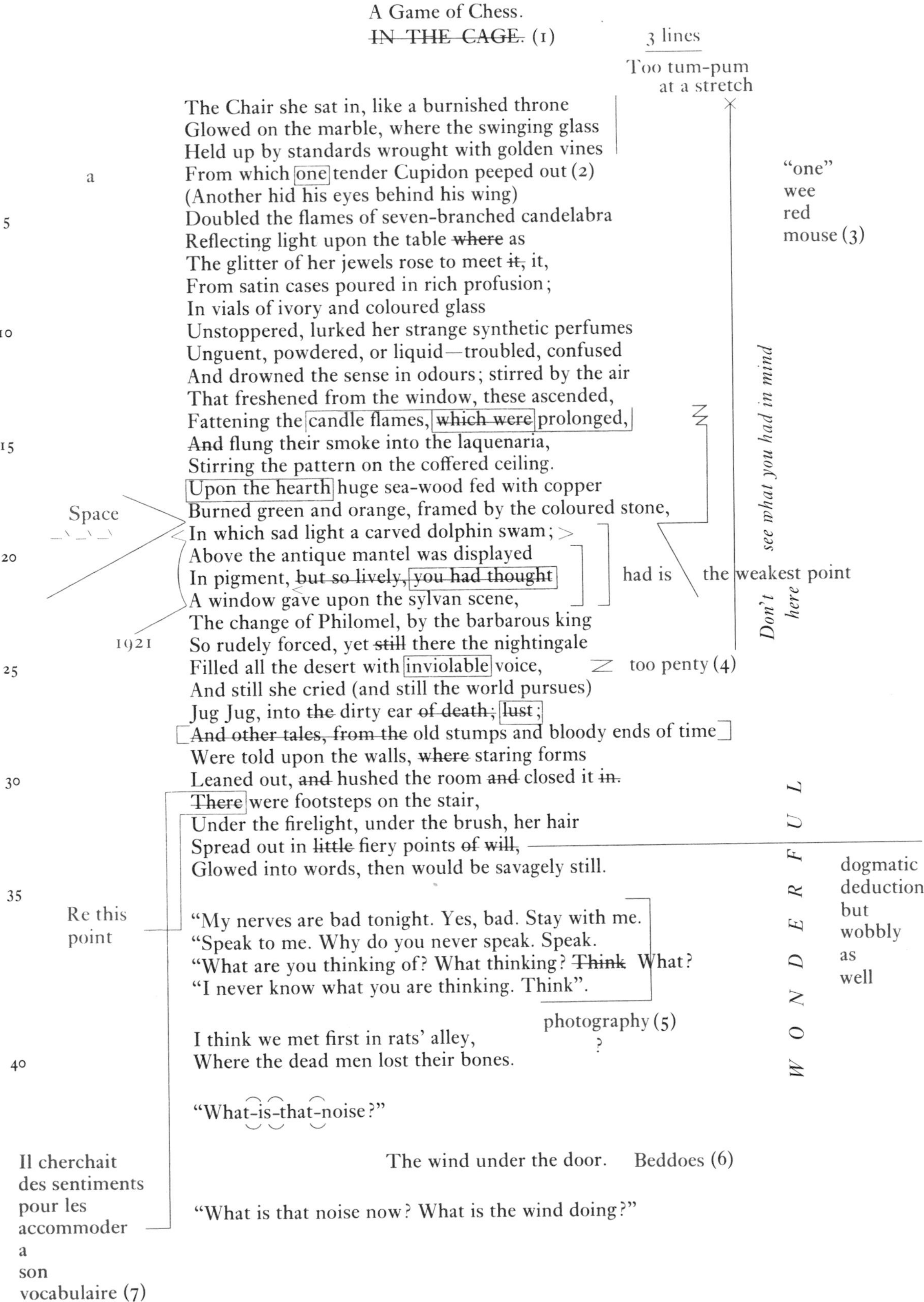

A Game of Chess.
~~IN THE CAGE.~~ (1)

3 lines
Too tum-pum at a stretch

The Chair she sat in, like a burnished throne
Glowed on the marble, where the swinging glass
Held up by standards wrought with golden vines
From which one tender Cupidon peeped out (2)
(Another hid his eyes behind his wing)
Doubled the flames of seven-branched candelabra
Reflecting light upon the table ~~where~~ as
The glitter of her jewels rose to meet ~~it,~~ it,
From satin cases poured in rich profusion;
In vials of ivory and coloured glass
Unstoppered, lurked her strange synthetic perfumes
Unguent, powdered, or liquid—troubled, confused
And drowned the sense in odours; stirred by the air
That freshened from the window, these ascended,
Fattening the candle flames, ~~which were~~ prolonged,
~~And~~ flung their smoke into the laquenaria,
Stirring the pattern on the coffered ceiling.
Upon the hearth huge sea-wood fed with copper
Burned green and orange, framed by the coloured stone,
In which sad light a carved dolphin swam;
Above the antique mantel was displayed
In pigment, ~~but so lively,~~ ~~you had thought~~
A window gave upon the sylvan scene,
The change of Philomel, by the barbarous king
So rudely forced, yet ~~still~~ there the nightingale
Filled all the desert with inviolable voice,
And still she cried (and still the world pursues)
Jug Jug, into ~~the~~ dirty ear ~~of death;~~ lust;
~~And other tales, from the~~ old stumps and bloody ends of time
Were told upon the walls, ~~where~~ staring forms
Leaned out, ~~and~~ hushed the room ~~and~~ closed it ~~in.~~
~~There~~ were footsteps on the stair,
Under the firelight, under the brush, her hair
Spread out in ~~little~~ fiery points ~~of will,~~
Glowed into words, then would be savagely still.

"My nerves are bad tonight. Yes, bad. Stay with me.
"Speak to me. Why do you never speak. Speak.
"What are you thinking of? What thinking? ~~Think~~ What?
"I never know what you are thinking. Think".

I think we met first in rats' alley,
Where the dead men lost their bones.

"What-is-that-noise?"

The wind under the door. Beddoes (6)

"What is that noise now? What is the wind doing?"

a

"one" wee red mouse (3)

Space

1921

had is the weakest point

Don't see what you had in mind here

too penty (4)

W O N D E R F U L

dogmatic deduction but wobbly as well

Re this point

photography (5) ?

Il cherchait des sentiments pour les accommoder a son vocabulaire (7)

Typescript on three leaves of this section, with Eliot's additions, and Vivien Eliot's comments, in pencil. Pound's criticism is in pencil and in ink. Line 16: laquenaria] laquearia.

Carrying
Away the little light dead people.

"You know nothing? Do you see nothing? Do you remember
"Nothing?"

I remember
The hyacinth garden. Those are pearls that were his eyes, yes!

"Are you alive, or not? Is there nothing in your head?"

But

O O O O that Shakespeherian Rag-
It's so elegant-
So intelligent-

"What shall I do now? What shall I do?
"I shall rush out as I am, and walk the street
"With my hair down, so. What shall we do tomorrow?
"What shall we ever do?"

The hot water at ten.
And if it rains, the closed carriage at four.
And we shall play a game of chess:
The ivory men make company between us
Pressing lidless eyes and waiting for a knock upon the door.

When Lil's husband was coming back out of the Transport Corps
I didn't mince my words, I said to her myself,
HURRY UP PLEASE IT'S TIME.
"Now Albert's coming back, make yourself a bit smart.
"He'll want to know what you did with that money he gave you
"To get yourself some teeth". He did, I was there.
"You have them all out, Lil, and get a nice set",
He said, "I swear, I can't bear to look at you".
"And no more can I", I said, "and think of poor Albert,
"He's been in the army four years, he wants a good time,
"And if you don't give it him, there's many another will".
"Other women", she said. "Something o' that", I said.
"Then I'll know who to thank", she said, and gave me a straight l
HURRY UP PLEASE IT'S TIME.
"No, ma'am, you needn't look old-fashioned at me", I said,
"Others can pick and choose if you can't.
"But if Albert makes off, it won't be for lack of telling.
You ought to be ashamed," I said, "to look so antique".
-(And her only thirty-one).
"I can't help it", she said, putting on a long face,
"It's that medicine I took, in order to bring it off."
(She's had five already, and nearly died of young George).
"The chemist said it would be allright, but I've never been the s
"You are a proper fool", I said.
"Well if Albert won't leave you alone, there it is", I said.

Carrying
Away the little light dead people. (1)

"Do?
"~~Do~~ You know nothing? Do you see nothing? Do you remember
"Nothing?"

wonderful

I remember
The hyacinth garden. Those are pearls that were his eyes, ~~yes!~~   Penelope (2)
J. J.

"Are you alive, or not? Is there nothing in your head?"
photo.

But
O O O O that Shakespeherian Rag—
It's so elegant—
So intelligent—

"What shall I do now? What shall I do?
"I shall rush out as I am, and walk the street
"With my hair down, so. What shall we do tomorrow?
"What shall we ever do?"

& wonderful

Why this Blot on Scutchen between 1922 & Lil[1]

bottle!
The hot water at ten.
And if it rains, the closed carriage (3) at four.
And we shall play a game of chess:
The ivory men make company between us (4)
Pressing lidless eyes and waiting for a knock upon the door.

1880

Yes

~~Discharge out of the army~~??
demobbed
When Lil's husband was ~~coming back out of the~~ ~~Transport Corps~~ ?
I didn't mince my words, I said to her myself,
HURRY UP PLEASE IT'S TIME.
"Now Albert's coming back, make yourself a bit smart. (5)
"He'll want to know what you did with that money he gave you
"To get yourself some teeth". He did, I was there.
"You have them all out, Lil, and get a nice set",
He said, "I swear, I can't bear to look at you".
"And no more can I", I said, "and think of poor Albert,
"He's been in the army four years, he wants a good time,
"And if you don't give it him, there's many another will".
("Other women") she said. "Something of that", I said.
"Then I'll know who to thank", she said, and gave me a straight look.
HURRY UP PLEASE IT'S TIME.
~~"No, ma'am, you needn't look old-fashioned at~~ me", I said,
"Others can pick and choose if you can't.
"But if Albert makes off, it won't be for lack of telling.
"You ought to be ashamed," I said, "to look so antique".
—(And her only thirty-one).
"I can't help it", she said, putting on a long face,
"It's that ~~medicine~~ I took, ~~in order~~ to bring it off".
(She's had five already, and nearly died of young George).
"The chemist said it would be all right, but I've never been the same".
"You *are* a proper fool", I said.
"Well if Albert won't leave you alone, there it is", I said.

Perhaps better not so soon. C[ou]ld you put this later.

I want to avoid trying show pronunciation by spelling

Or If you dont like it you can get on with it

~~stuff~~ pills

Lines 45–6, 63, and the first three words of line 50, are unpublished.

* ~~"You want to keep him at home, I suppose"~~.
HURRY UP PLEASE IT'S TIME.
Well that Sunday Albert was home, they had a hot gammon,
And they asked me in to dinner, to get the beauty of it hot-
HURRY UP PLEASE IT'S TIME.
HURRY UP PLEASE IT'S TIME.
Good night, Bill. Good night, Lou. Good night, George. Good night.
Ta ta. ~~Good night.~~ Good night.
Good night, ladies, good night, sweet ladies, good night, good night.

Splendid last lines

X What you get married for if you don't want to have children

3

✳ ~~"You want to keep him at home, I suppose".~~
HURRY UP PLEASE IT'S TIME.
Well that Sunday Albert was home, they had a hot gammon,
And they asked me in to dinner, to get the beauty of it hot—
HURRY UP PLEASE IT'S TIME.
HURRY UP PLEASE IT'S TIME.
Goo~~d~~ night, Bill. Goo~~d~~ night, Lou. Goo~~d~~ night, George. Goo~~d~~ night.
Ta ta. ~~Good night. Good night.~~
Good night, ladies, good night, sweet ladies, good night, good night.
Splendid last lines

✳ *What you get married for if you*
dont want to have children

On the verso of this leaf, Vivien Eliot has written in pencil to her husband: 'Make any of these alterations—or *none* if you prefer. Send me back this copy & let me have it.'

HE DO THE POLICE IN DIFFERENT VOICES: Part II.

~~IN THE CAGE.~~ A game of Chess.

The Chair she sat in, like a burnished throne
Glowed on the marble, where the swinging glass
Held up by standards wrought with golden vines
From which one tender Cupidon peeped out
(Another hid his eyes behind his wing)
Doubled the flames of seven-branched candelabra
Reflecting light upon the table ~~where~~ as
The glitter of her jewels rose to meet ~~it~~ it,
From satin cases poured in rich profusion;
In vials of ivory and coloured glass
Unstoppered, lurked her strange synthetic perfumes
Unguent, powdered, or liquid- troubled, confused
And drowned the sense in odours; stirred by the air
That freshened from the window, these ascended,
Fattening the candle flames, which were prolonged,
And flung their smoke into the laquenaria,
Stirring the pattern on the coffered ceiling.
Upon the hearth huge sea-wood fed with copper
Burned green and orange, framed by the coloured stone,
In which sad light a carved dolphin swam;
Above the antique mantel was displayed
In pigment, but so lively, you had thought
A window gave upon the sylvan scene,
The change of Philomel, by the barbarous king
So rudely forced, yet ~~still~~ there the nightingale
Filled all the desert with inviolable voice,
And still she cried (and still the world pursues)
Jug Jug, into the dirty ear of death;
And other tales, from the old stumps and bloody ends of time
Were told upon the walls, where staring forms
Leaned out, and hushed the room and closed it in.
There were footsteps on the stair,
Under the firelight, under the brush, her hair
Spread out in little fiery points of will,
Glowed into words, then would be savagely still.

"My nerves are bad tonight. Yes, bad. Stay with me.
"Speak to me. Why do you never speak. Speak.
"What are you thinking of? What thinking? ~~Think~~ What?
"I never know what you are thinking. Think".

I think we met first in rats' alley,
Where the dead men lost their bones.

"What is that noise?"

The wind under the door.

"What is that noise now? What is the wind doing?"

HE DO THE POLICE IN DIFFERENT VOICES: Part II.

A Game of Chess.
~~IN THE CAGE.~~

The Chair she sat in, like a burnished throne
Glowed on the marble, where the swinging glass
Held up by standards wrought with golden vines
From which one tender Cupidon peeped out
(Another hid his eyes behind his wing)
Doubled the flames of seven-branched candelabra
Reflecting light upon the table ~~where~~ as
The glitter of her jewels rose to meet ~~it,~~ it,
From satin cases poured in rich profusion;
In vials of ivory and coloured glass
Unstoppered, lurked her strange synthetic perfumes
Unguent, powdered, or liquid—troubled, confused
And drowned the sense in odours; stirred by the air
That freshened from the window, these ascended,
Fattening the candle flames, which were prolonged,
And flung their smoke into the laquenaria,
Stirring the pattern on the coffered ceiling.
Upon the hearth huge sea-wood fed with copper
Burned green and orange, framed by the coloured stone,
In which sad light a carved dolphin swam;
Above the antique mantel was displayed
In pigment, but so lively, you had thought
A window gave upon the sylvan scene,
The change of Philomel, by the barbarous king
So rudely forced, yet ~~still~~ there the nightingale
Filled all the desert with inviolable voice,
And still she cried (and still the world pursues)
Jug Jug, into the dirty ear of death;
And other tales, from the old stumps and bloody ends of time
Were told upon the walls, where staring forms
Leaned out, and hushed the room and closed it in.
There were footsteps on the stair,
Under the firelight, under the brush, her hair
Spread out in little fiery points of will,
Glowed into words, then would be savagely still.

"My nerves are bad tonight. Yes, bad. Stay with me.
"Speak to me. Why do you never speak. Speak.
"What are you thinking of? What thinking? ~~Think~~ What?
"I never know what you are thinking. Think".

I think we met first in rats' alley,
Where the dead men lost their bones.

"What is that noise?"
The wind under the door.

"What is that noise now? What is the wind doing?"

Carbon of the typescript on which Eliot has noted, in pencil, some of his wife's suggestions.
Line 16: laquenaria] laquearia.

Carrying
Away the little light dead people.

"Do you know nothing? Do you see nothing? Do you remember
"Nothing?"

I remember
The hyacinth garden. Those are pearls that were his eyes, yes!

"Are you alive, or not? Is there nothing in your head?"

But
O O O O that Shakespeherian Rag-
It's so elegant-
So intelligent-

"What shall I do now? What shall I do?
"I shall rush out as I am, and walk the street
"With my hair down, so. What shall we do tomorrow?
"What shall we ever do?"

The hot water at ten.
And if it rains, the closed carriage at four.
And we shall play a game of chess:
The ivory men make company between us
Pressing lidless eyes and waiting for a knock upon the door.

When Lil's husband was coming back out of the Transport Corps
I didn't mince my words, I said to her myself,
HURRY UP PLEASE IT'S TIME.
"Now Albert's coming back, make yourself a bit smart.
"He'll want to know what you did with that money he gave you
"To get yourself some teeth". He did, he was there.
"You have them all out, Lil, and get a nice set",
He said, "I swear, I can't bear to look at you".
"And no more can I", I said, "and think of poor Albert,
"He's been in the army four years, he wants a good time,
"And if you don't give it him, there's many another will".
"Other women", she said. "Something of that", I said.
"Then I'll know who to thank", she said, and gave me a straight
HURRY UP PLEASE IT'S TIME.
"No, ~~ma'am~~, you needn't look old-fashioned at me", I said,
"Others can pick and choose if you can't.
"But if Albert makes off, it won't be for lack of telling.
"You ought to be ashamed," I said, "to look so antique".
-(And her only thirty-one).
"I can't help it", she said, putting on a long face,
"It's that medicine I took, in order to bring it off."
(She's had five already, and nearly died of young George).
"The chemist said it would be allright, but I've never been the
"You are a proper fool", I said.
"Well if Albert won't leave you alone, there it is", I said.

Carrying
Away the little light dead people.

"Do you know nothing? Do you see nothing? Do you remember
"Nothing?"

I remember
The hyacinth garden. Those are pearls that were his eyes, yes!

"Are you alive, or not? Is there nothing in your head?"

But
O O O O that Shakespeherian Rag—
It's so elegant—
So intelligent—

"What shall I do now? What shall I do?
"I shall rush out as I am, and walk the street
"With my hair down, so. What shall we do tomorrow?
"What shall we ever do?"

The hot water at ten.
And if it rains, the closed carriage at four.
And we shall play a game of chess:
The ivory men make company between us
Pressing lidless eyes and waiting for a knock upon the door.

When Lil's husband was coming back out of the Transport Corps
I didn't mince my words, I said to her myself,
HURRY UP PLEASE IT'S TIME.
"Now Albert's coming back, make yourself a bit smart.
"He'll want to know what you did with that money he gave you
"To get yourself some teeth". He did, I was there.
later? "You have them all out, Lil, and get a nice set",
He said, "I swear, I can't bear to look at you".
"And no more can I", I said, "and think of poor Albert,
"He's been in the army four years, he wants a good time,
"And if you don't give it him, there's many another will".
"Other women", she said. "Something of that", I said.
"Then I'll know who to thank", she said, and gave me a straight look.
HURRY UP PLEASE IT'S TIME.
If you dont like it you can get on with it
"No, ~~ma'am,~~ you needn't look old-fashioned at me", I said,
"Others can pick and choose if you can't.
"But if Albert makes off, it won't be for lack of telling.
"You ought to be ashamed," I said, "to look so antique".
—(And her only thirty-one).
"I can't help it", she said, putting on a long face,
"It's that medicine I took, in order to bring it off".
(She's had five already, and nearly died of young George).
"The chemist said it would be all right, but I've never been the same"
"You are a proper fool", I said.
"Well if Albert won't leave you alone, there it is", I said.

~~"You want to keep him at home, I suppose".~~
HURRY UP PLEASE IT'S TIME.
Well that Sunday Albert was home, they had a hot gammon,
And they asked me in to dinner, to get the beauty of it hot-
HURRY UP PLEASE IT'S TIME.
HURRY UP PLEASE IT'S TIME.
Good night, Bill. Good night, Lou. Good night, George. Good night.
Ta ta. Good night. Good night.
Good night, ladies, good night, sweet ladies, good night, good night.

What you get married for if you don't want to have children -

3

~~"You want to keep him at home, I suppose".~~
HURRY UP PLEASE IT'S TIME.
Well that Sunday Albert was home, they had a hot gammon,
And they asked me in to dinner, to get the beauty of it hot—
HURRY UP PLEASE IT'S TIME.
HURRY UP PLEASE IT'S TIME.
Good night, Bill. Good night, Lou. Good night, George. Good night.
Ta ta. Good night. Good night.
Good night, ladies, good night, sweet ladies, good night, good night.

What you
get married for
if you don't
want to have
children

THE FIRE SERMON.

Admonished by the sun's inclining ray,
~~And swift approaches of the thievish day,~~
The white-armed Fresca blinks, and yawns, and gapes,
Aroused from dreams of love and pleasant rapes.
Electric summons of the busy bell
Brings brisk Amanda to destroy the spell;
With coarsened hand, and hard plebeian tread,
Who draws the curtain round the lacquered bed,
Depositing thereby a polished tray
Of soothing chocolate, or stimulating tea.

Leaving the bubbling beverage to cool,
Fresca slips softly to the needful stool,
Where the pathetic tale of Richardson
Eases her labour till the deed is done.
Then slipping back between the conscious sheets,
Explores a ~~page of Gibbon~~ as she eats. the Daily Mirror
Her hands caress the egg's well-rounded dome,
She sinks in revery, till the letters come.
Their scribbled contents at a glance devours,
Then to reply devotes her practic'd powers.

"My dear, how are you? I'm unwell today,
And have been, since I saw you at the play.
I hope that nothing mars your gaity,
And things go better with you, than with me.
I went last night - more out of dull despair -
To Lady Kleinwurm's party - who was there?
Oh, Lady Kleinwurm's monde - no one that mattered -
Somebody sang, and Lady Kleinwurm chattered.
What are you reading? anything that's new?
I have a clever book by Giraudoux.
Clever, I think, is all. I've much to say -
But cannot say it - that is just my way -
When shall we meet - tell me all your manoeuvers;
And all about yourself and your new lovers -
And when to Paris? I must make an end,
My dear, believe me, your devoted
friend".

This ended, to the steaming bath she moves,
Her tresses fanned by little flutt'ring Loves;
Odours, confected by the ~~cunning~~ French, artful
Disguise the good old hearty female stench.

THE FIRE SERMON. (1)

Admonished by the sun's inclining ray,
? ~~And swift approaches of the thievish day,~~
~~Our~~ The white-armed Fresca (2) blinks, and yawns, and gapes, (3)
Aroused from dreams of love and pleasant rapes.
Electric summons of the busy bell
Brings brisk Amanda to destroy the spell;
With coarsened hand, and hard plebeian tread,
Who draws the curtain round the lacquered bed,
Depositing thereby a polished tray
Of soothing chocolate, or stimulating tea.

Leaving the bubbling beverage to cool,
Fresca slips softly to the needful stool,
Where the pathetic tale of Richardson (4)
Eases her labour till the deed is done.
Then slipping back between the conscious sheets,
Explores a ~~page of Gibbon~~ as she eats. the Daily Mirror
Her hands caress the egg's well-rounded dome,
She sinks in revery, till the letters come.
Their scribbled contents at a glance devours,
Then to reply devotes her practic'd powers.

"My dear, how are you? I'm unwell today,
And have been, since I saw you at the play.
I hope that nothing mars your gaity,
And things go better with you, than with me.
I went last night—more out of dull despair—
To Lady Kleinwurm's party—who was there?
Oh, Lady Kleinwurm's monde—no one that mattered—
Somebody sang, and Lady Kleinwurm chattered.
What are you reading? anything that's new?
I have a clever book by Giraudoux.
Clever, I think, is all. I've much to say—
But cannot say it—that is just my way—
When shall we meet—tell me all your manoeuvers;
And all about yourself and your new lovers—
And when to Paris? I must make an end,
My dear, believe me, your devoted
friend".

This ended, to the steaming bath she moves,
Her tresses fanned by little flutt'ring Loves;
Odours, confected by the ~~cunning~~ French,
Disguise the good old ~~female stench~~./hearty female stench.
artful

Typescript on five leaves, with pencilled revisions, and Pound's marginalia in ink. Lines 1–70 are unpublished, but see note (3) for Vivien Eliot's use of an earlier draft containing line 17.

The river's tent is broken & the last fingers of leaf
Clutch & sink into the wet bank. The wind
Crosses the brown land, unheard. The nymphs are departed.
(Sweet Thames etc.)

The river bears no empty bottles, sandwich papers,
Newspapers, cardboard boxes, cigarette ends
Or other testimony of ~~summer~~ nights. The nymphs are departed.
(And their friends, the loitering heirs of City directors
Departed, and left no addresses.
By the waters

The rivers tent is broken and the last fingers of leaf
Clutch and sink into the wet bank. The wind
Crosses the brown land, unheard. The nymphs are departed
(Sweet Thames etc).
The river bears no empty bottles, sandwich papers
~~Ca~~/Newspapers, cardboard boxes, cigarette ends
Or other testimony of summer nights.
The nymphs are departed.
(And their friends, the loitering heirs of City directors)
Departed, and left no addresses.
By the waters

Verso of leaf. First draft, in pencil, of what became the opening lines (173–82) of 'The Fire Sermon'.

Fresca! in other time or place had been
A meek and ~~lowly~~ weeping Magdalene;
More sinned against than sinning, bruised and marred,
The lazy laughing Jenny of the bard.
(The same eternal and consuming itch
Can make a martyr, or plain simple bitch);
Or prudent sly domestic puss puss cat,
Or autumn's favourite in a furnished flat,
Or strolling slattern in a tawdry gown,
A doorstep dunged by every dog in town.
For varying forms, one definition's right:
Unreal emotions, and real appetite.
Women ~~grown~~ intellectual grow dull,
And lose the mother wit of natural trull.
Fresca was ~~baptized in~~ a soapy sea
Of Symonds- Walter Pater- Vernon Lee.
The Scandinavians bemused her wits,
The Russians thrilled her to hysteric fits.
From ~~For~~ such chaotic misch-masch potpourri
What are we to expect but poetry?
When restless nights distract her brain from sleep
She may as well write poetry, as count sheep.
And on those nights when Fresca lies alone,
She scribbles verse of such a gloomy tone
That cautious critics say, her style is quite her own.
Not quite an adult, and still less a child,
By fate misbred, by flattering friends beguiled,
Fresca's arrived (the Muses Nine declare)
To be a sort of can-can salonniere.
But at my back from time to time I hear
The rattle of the bones, and chuckle spread from ear to ear.

A rat crept softly through the vegetation
Dragging its slimy belly on the bank
While I was fishing in the dull canal
On a winter evening round behind the gashouse,
Musing upon the king my brother's wreck
And on the king my father's death before him.
White bodies naked on the low damp ground,
And bones cast in a little low dry garret,
Rattled by the rat's foot only, year to year.
But at my back from time to time I hear
The sound of horns and motors, which shall bring
Sweeney to Mrs.Porter in the spring.
O the moon shone bright on Mrs.Porter
And on her daughter
They wash their feet in soda water
Et O ces voix d'enfants, chantant dans la coupole!

2

Fresca! in other time or place had been
A meek and ~~lowly~~ weeping Magdalene;
More sinned against than sinning, (1) bruised and marred,
The lazy laughing Jenny of the bard. (2)
(The same eternal and consuming itch
Can make a martyr, or plain simple bitch);
Or prudent sly domestic puss puss cat,
Now ~~Or~~ autumn's favourite in a furnished flat,
Or strolling slattern in a tawdry gown,
A doorstep dunged by every dog in town.
For varying forms, one definition's right:
Unreal emotions, and real appetite.
But Women ~~grown~~ intellectual grow dull,
And lose the mother wit of natural trull.
Fresca was ~~baptised in~~ a soapy sea
born upon Of Symonds—Walter Pater—Vernon Lee. (3) insert *
The Scandinavians bemused her wits,
The Russians thrilled her to hysteric fits.
From ~~For~~ such chaotic misch-masch potpourri
What are we to expect but poetry?
When restless nights distract her brain from sleep
She may as well write poetry, as count sheep.
And on those nights when Fresca ~~lies~~ alone,
She scribbles verse ~~of~~ such a gloomy tone
That cautious critics say, her style is quite her own.
Not quite an adult, and still less a child,
By fate misbred, by flattering friends beguiled,
Fresca's arrived (the Muses Nine declare)
To be a sort of can-can salonnière. (4)
But at my back from time to time I hear
The rattle of the bones, and chuckle spread from ear to ear.

surely
as you are
writing of
London
this
adj.
is tauto.

A rat crept softly through the vegetation
Dragging its slimy belly on the bank
While I was fishing in the dull canal
On a winter evening round behind the gashouse,
O.K. Musing upon the king my brother's wreck
And on the king my father's death before him.
White bodies naked on the low damp ground,
And bones cast in a little low dry garret,
Rattled by the rat's foot only, year to year.
But at my back from time to time I hear
The sound of horns and motors, which shall bring
Sweeney to Mrs. Porter in the spring.
O the moon shone bright on Mrs. Porter
And on her daughter
They wash their feet in soda water
Et O ces voix d'enfants, chantant dans la coupole!

STET

See next page for insertion.
Line 71, adapted, became line 185. Lines 72–88 became lines 186–202.

* From which, a Venus Anadyomene
She stept ashore to a more varied scene,
Propelled by Lady Katzegg's guiding hand
She knew the wealth and fashion of the land,
Among the fame and beauty of the stage
She passed, the wonder of our little age,
She gave the turf her intellectual patronage.
But F. rules ~~She reigns~~ even more ~~no less~~ distinguished spheres,
Minerva in a crowd of boxing peers.
Aeneas' mother, with an altered face,
Appeared ~~once~~ reached him in ~~unexpected~~ unfamiliar place:
He ~~recognised~~ knew ~~the~~ goddess by her ~~[illegible]~~ celestial pace.
~~He knew the goddess by her smooth celestial pace~~
So the [illegible] in the cinema
Identify ~~Know [illegible]~~ a goddess or a star.
~~[illegible]~~ In silent rapture worship from afar.
Thus art ennobles even wealth and birth,
And breeding raises prostrate art from earth.

To Aeneas, in an unfamiliar place,
Appeared his mother, with an altered face,
He knew the goddess by her smooth celestial pa

* From which, a Venus Anadyomene
She stept ashore to a more varied scene,
Propelled by Lady Katzegg's guiding hand
She knew the wealth and fashion of the land,
Among the fame and beauty of the stage
She passed, the wonder of our little age; (1)
She gave the turf her intellectual patronage.

~~governs~~
But F. rules ~~dominates~~ even more
~~She reigns~~ ~~no less~~ distinguished spheres,
Minerva in a crowd of boxing peers. (2)

Aeneas' mother, with an altered face,
roached him unfamiliar
App~~eared once~~ in an ~~unexpected~~ place:
knew ~~divinity's celestial pace~~
He ~~recognised the goddess by her supernatural grace~~
the goddess by her smooth celestial pace. (3)

~~pact~~
So the ~~close~~ ~~millions~~
close rabble
~~The sweating rabble~~ in the cinema
~~thousands~~,

Identify ~~Know~~ ~~Sees on the screen,~~
~~Can recognise~~ a goddess or a star.

silent rapture
~~In reverent~~ In ~~reverent~~ ~~heaven~~
~~And hushed silence silence~~ worships ^ from afar.
Thus art ennobles even wealth and birth,
And breeding raises prostrate art from earth.

To Aeneas, in an unfamiliar place,
Appeared his mother, with an altered face,
He knew the goddess by her smooth celestial pace.

Insertion for previous page. First draft, in pencil. Unpublished. Line 13: pact = packed.

Twit twit twit twit twit twit twit
Tereu tereu
So rudely forc'd.
Ter

Unreal City, I have seen and see
Under the brown fog of your winter noon
Mr.Eugenides, the Smyrna merchant,
Unshaven, with a pocket full of currants
(C.i.f. London: documents at sight),
Who asked me, in ~~abominable~~ French,
To luncheon at the Cannon Street Hotel,
And perhaps a weekend at the Metropole.

Twit twit twit
Jug jug jug jug jug jug
Tereu
O swallow swallow
Ter

London, the swarming life you kill and breed,
~~Huddled between the concrete and the sky,~~
Responsive to the momentary need,
Vibrates unconscious to its formal destiny,

~~Knowing neither how to think, nor how to feel,~~
~~But~~ lives in the ~~awareness~~ of the observ~~ing~~ eye.
~~Londonxyourxpeoplexisxboundxuponxthexwheelx~~
~~Phantasmal gnomes, burrowing in brick and stone and steel!~~
Some minds, aberrant from the normal equipoise
~~(London, your people is bound upon the wheel!)~~
Record the motions of these pavement toys
And trace the cryptogram that may be curled
Within these faint perceptions of the noise,
Of the movement, and the lights!

Not here, O ~~Ademantus~~ Glaucon, but in another world.

At the violet hour, the hour when eyes and back and hand
Turn upward from the desk, the human engine waits -
Like a taxi throbbing waiting at a stand -
~~To spring to pleasure through the horn or ivory gates,~~

I Tiresias, though blind, throbbing between two lives,
Old man with wrinkled female breasts, can see
At the violet hour, the evening hour that strives
Homeward, and brings the sailor home from sea,

Twit twit twit twit twit twit twit
Tereu tereu
So rudely forc'd.
Ter

Unreal City, (I have seen and see)
Under the brown fog of your winter noon
Mr. Eugenides, the Smyrna merchant,
-en or -ed Unshaven, with a pocket full of currants
(C.i.f. London: documents at sight),
Who asked me, in ~~abominable~~ French, ? ~~his vile~~ / demotic
To luncheon at the Cannon Street Hotel,
And perhaps a weekend at the Metropole. dam per'apsez

Twit twit twit
Jug jug jug jug jug jug
Tereu
O swallow swallow
Ter

London, the swarming life you kill and breed, B ll S
~~Huddled between the concrete and the sky;~~
Responsive to the momentary need,
Vibrates unconscious to its formal destiny, keep

~~Knowing neither how to think, nor how to feel,~~ transformations
~~But~~ lives in the ~~awareness~~ of the observ~~ing~~ eye. ant
~~London, your people is bound upon the wheel~~! ~~only~~
~~Phantasmal gnomes, burrowing in brick and stone and steel~~!
Some minds, aberrant from the normal equipoise Palmer Cox's (1) brownies
~~(London, your people is bound upon the wheel!)~~
Record the motions of these pavement toys
And trace the cryptogram that may be curled
Within ~~these~~ faint perceptions of the noise,
Of the movement, and the lights!

Not here, O ~~Ademantus~~ Glaucon, but in another world. (2)

At the violet hour, the hour when eyes and back and hand
Turn upward from the desk, the human engine waits—
Like a taxi throbbing waiting at a stand—
~~To spring to pleasure through the horn or ivory gates,~~ (3)

I Tiresias, though blind, throbbing between two lives,
Old man with wrinkled female breasts, can see
At the violet hour, the evening hour that strives
Homeward, and brings the sailor home from sea,

Lines 89–90, 92, 105–20, and 124 are unpublished. Line 104 became part of line 428.
Line 96: 'Unshaven'. Not surprisingly Pound thought Eliot had typed 'Unshavan'.
Line 120: Ademantus = Adeimantus.

The typist home at teatime, who begins
To clear her broken breakfast away her broken breakfast, lights
Her stove, and lays out squalid food in tins,
Prepares the ~~room~~ and sets the room to rights.
toast

Out of the window perilously spread
Her drying combinations meet the sun's last rays,
And on the divan piled, (at night her bed),
Are stockings, dirty camisoles, and stays.

vide Mr. Sweeney
Vide Mr. Pope

A bright kimono wraps her as she sprawls
In nerveless torpor on the window seat;
A touch of art is given by the false
Japanese print, purchased in Oxford Street.

I Tiresias, old man with wrinkled dugs,
Perceived the scene, and foretold the rest,
Knowing the manner of these crawling bugs,
I too awaited the expected guest.

A youth of twentyone, spotted about the face,
One of those simple loiterers whom we say
We may have seen in any public place
At almost any hour of night or day.

Pride has not fired him with ambitious rage,
His hair is thick with grease, and thick with scurf,
Perhaps his inclinations touch the stage -
Not sharp enough to ~~associate~~ with the turf.
mingle

~~He, the young man carbuncular, will stare~~
~~Boldly about, in "London's one cafe",~~
~~And he will tell her, with a casual air,~~
~~Grandly, "I have been with Nevinson today".~~

or ~~Perhaps~~ else a cheap house agent's clerk, who flits
Daily, from flat to flat, with one bold stare;
One of the low on whom assurance sits
As a silk hat on a Bradford millionaire.

He munches with the same peristent stare,
He knows his way with women and that's that!
Impertinently tilting back his chair
And dropping cigarette ash on the mat.

The time is now propitious, as he guesses,
The meal is ended, she is bored and tired;
Endeavours to engage her in caresses,
Which still are unreproved, if undesired.

4

The typist home at teatime, who begins
To clear ~~her broken breakfast~~ away her broken breakfast, lights
Her stove, and lays out squalid food in tins,
Prepares the ~~room~~ and sets the room to rights.
toast
Out of the window perilously spread — vide
Her drying combinations meet the sun's last rays, — other
And on the divan piled, (at night her bed), — copy*
Are stockings, dirty camisoles, and stays.

A bright kimono wraps her as she sprawls
In nerveless torpor on the window seat;
A touch of art is given by the false
Japanese print, purchased in Oxford Street.

I Tiresias, old man with wrinkled dugs,
Perceived the scene, and foretold the rest,
Knowing the manner of these crawling bugs,
I too awaited the expected guest.

A youth of twentyone, spotted about the face,
One of those simple loiterers whom we say
We may have seen in any public place
At ~~almost any hour of night or~~ day.

Pride has not fired him with ambitious rage,
His hair is thick with grease, and thick with scurf,
Perhaps his inclinations touch the stage—
Not sharp enough to ~~associate~~ with the turf.
mingle
~~He, the young man carbuncular, will stare~~
~~Boldly about, in "London's one cafe", (1)~~
~~And he will tell her, with a casual air,~~
~~Grandly, "I have been with Nevinson (2) today".~~

else
Or ~~Perhaps~~ a cheap house agent's clerk, who flits
Daily, from flat to flat, with one bold stare;
One of the low on whom assurance sits
As a silk hat on a Bradford millionaire.

He munches with the same persistent stare,
He knows his way with women and that's that!
Impertinently tilting back his chair
And dropping cigarette ash on the mat.

The time is now propitious, as he guesses,
The meal is ended, she is bored and tired;
Endeavours to engage her in caresses,
Which still are unreproved, if undesired.

Lines 132, 137–40, 143, 145–52, 154–6, and 161–4 are unpublished.
* Page 45.

Flushed and decided, he assaults at once,
Exploring hands encounter no defence;
His vanity requires no response,
And makes a welcome of indifference.

(And I Tiresias have foresuffered all
Enacted on this same divan or bed,
I who have sat by Thebes beneath the wall
And walked among the lowest of the dead).

-Bestows one final patronising kiss,
And gropes his way, finding the stairs unlit;
And at the corner where the stable is,
Delays only to urinate, and spit.

She turns and looks a moment in the glass,
Hardly aware of her departed lover;
Across her brain one half-formed thought may pass:
"Well now that's done, and I'm glad it's over".

. . . .

When lovely woman stoops to folly and
Paces moves about her room again, alone,
She smoothes her hair with automatic hand,
And puts a record on the gramophone.

"This music crept by me upon the waters"
And along the Strand, ~~and~~ up Queen Victoria ~~theghastly hill of Cannon~~ Street,
Fading at last, ~~behind~~ ~~my~~ flying feet,
There where the tower was traced against the night
Of Michael Paternoster Royal, red and white.

5.

Flushed and decided, he assaults at once,
Exploring hands encounter no defence;
His vanity requires no response,
And makes a welcome of indifference.

(And I Tiresias have foresuffered all
Enacted on this same divan or bed,
I who have sat by Thebes beneath the wall
And walked among the lowest of the dead.)

—Bestows one final patronising kiss,
And gropes his way, finding the stairs unlit;
And at the corner where the stable is,
Delays only to urinate, and spit.

She turns and looks a moment in the glass,
Hardly aware of her departed lover;
Across her brain one half-formed thought may pass:
"Well now that's done,—and I'~~am~~ glad it's over".

. . . .

When lovely woman stoops to folly and
Then ~~She~~ moves about her room again, alone,
She smoothes her hair with automatic hand,
And puts a record on the gramophone.

"This music crept by me upon the waters" Queen Victoria
And along the Strand, ~~and~~ up ~~the ghastly hill of Cannon~~ Street,
~~Fading~~ at last, ~~behind~~ by ~~flying~~ feet,
There where the tower was traced against the night
Of Michael Paternoster Royal, red and white. (1)

Lines 179–80 and 191–3 are unpublished.

1

O City, city, I have heard & hear
The pleasant whining of ~~the~~ a mandoline
Beside a public bar in Lower Thames Street
And a clatter & a chatter ~~with the~~ bar from within
Where fishmen lounge ~~[illegible]~~ at noon time; where the walls
Of Magnus Martyr stood, & stand, & hold
~~Inviolable~~ ~~Their joyful~~ Splendour of Corinthian white & gold
Inexplicable

London, the swarming life you kill & breed, ~~[illegible]~~
~~Swarming~~ ~~Staring~~ Huddled ~~[illegible]~~ stunned between the concrete & the sky
~~[illegible]~~ Responsive to the momentary need
Vibrates unconscious to its ~~their~~ formal ~~[illegible]~~ destiny
Knowing neither how ~~[illegible]~~ to think, nor how to feel,
But Lives ~~[illegible]~~ in the awareness of the observing eye;
~~Phantasmal~~ gnomes, burrowing ~~travelling~~ in brick & stone & steel!
Some minds, aberrant ~~[illegible]~~ from the natural equipoise
(London! your {populations / ~~people~~} is bound upon the wheel!)
Record the jerky motions ~~movements~~ of these pavement ~~huddled~~ toys
And trace the cryptogram ~~[illegible]~~ which may be curled
~~Distinct~~ ~~[illegible]~~ these faint perceptions
Within ~~the~~ ~~[illegible]~~ consciousness of the noise

1

O City, City, I have heard and hear
The pleasant whining of ~~the~~ a mandoline
~~Outside~~/Beside a public bar in lower Thames Street
And a clatter and a chatter ~~in the bar~~ from within
Where fishmen lounge ~~and loafe and spit at noon~~
time ~~out~~
at noon ^ ~~where~~/there the walls
Of Magnus Martyr stood, and stand, and hold
~~Inviolable~~ ~~music~~
~~Their joyful~~ { splendour of Corinthian white and gold
Inexplicable

---

you kill and breed and ~~feed~~
~~daily~~
life
London, the swarming ~~creatures~~ ~~that you breed~~
~~Scampering~~ ~~Striving~~ Huddled ~~dazed~~ the concrete and the
~~Among half stunned beneath~~/between ~~a heavy~~ sky
stunned
~~solely~~
~~Quickly~~ Responsive to the momentary need
its ~~their~~ formal
Vibrates unconscious to ~~their chords of~~ destiny;
neither how to nor how to
Knowing ~~little what they~~ think, ~~and muchless what they~~ feel,
But Lives ~~only~~/~~chiefly~~ in the awareness of the observing eye;
gnomes burrowing
~~Spectral~~/Phantasmal ~~goblins tunnelling~~ in brick and stone and steel!
minds aberrant
Some ~~brains,~~ ~~unbalanced~~ from the natural equipoise
population
(London! your { ~~pop~~/people is bound upon the wheel!)
pavement
jerky motions ~~poor cheap~~
Record the ~~movements~~ of these ~~huddled~~ toys
~~tarnished~~
cryptogram/~~s~~ may ~~is~~/be curled
And trace the ~~painful, ideal meaning~~ which ~~they spell~~
~~Indistinctly Vaguely~~
~~Doubtfully into~~ these faint perceptions
faint of the noise
Within ~~this~~ ~~penumbral~~ ~~s/consciousness~~

All in pencil.
'O City . . .' First draft of lines 259–65.
Line 5: loafe = loaf.
Line 7: Indecipherable squiggle after 'gold'.
'London . . .' First draft of the apostrophe (see p. 31).
Above line 6: 'bu[t]' or 'on[ly]'?

THE FIRE SERMON.

Admonished by the sun's inclining ray,
And swift approaches of the thievish day,
The white-armed Fresca blinks, and yawns, and gapes,
Aroused from dreams of love and pleasant rapes.
Electric summons of the busy bell
Bring brisk Amanda to destroy the spell;
With coarsened hand, and hard plebeian tread,
Who draws the curtain round the lacquered bed,
Depositing thereby a polished tray
Of soothing chocolate, or stimulating tea.

Leaving the bubbling beverage to cool,
Fresca slips softly to the needful stool,
Where the pathetic tale of Richardson
Eases her labour till the deed is done.
Then slipping back between the conscious sheets,
Explores a page of Gibbon as she eats.
Her hands caress the egg's well-rounded dome,
She sinks in revery, till the letters come.
Their scribbled contents at a glance devours,
Then to reply devotes her practic'd powers.

"My dear, how are you? I'm unwell today,
And have been, since I saw you at the play.
I hope that nothing mars your gaity,
And things go better with you, than with me.
I went last night - more out of dull despair -
To Lady Kleinwurm's party - who was there?
Oh, Lady Kleinwurm's monde - no one that mattered -
Somebody sang, and Lady Kleinwurm chattered.
What are you reading? anything that's new?
I have a clever book by Giraudoux.
Clever, I think, is all. I've much to say -
But cannot say it - that is just my way -
When shall we meet - tell me all your manoeuvers;
And all about yourself and your new lovers -
And when to Paris? I must make an end,
My dear, believe me, your devoted
friend".

This ended, to the steaming bath she moves,
Her tresses fanned by little flutt'ring Loves;
Odours, confected by the ~~cunning French~~,
Disguise the good old ~~Hearty Stench~~. stench.

?

Too loose

rhyme drags it out to diffuseness

trick of Pope etc not to let couple diffuse 'em.

THE FIRE SERMON.

1

Admonished by the sun's inclining ray,
And swift approaches of the thievish day,
The white-armed Fresca blinks, and yawns, and gapes,
Aroused from dreams of love and pleasant rapes.
Electric summons of the busy bell
Bring[s] brisk Amanda to destroy the spell;
With coarsened hand, and hard plebeian tread,
Who draws the curtain round the lacquered bed,
Depositing thereby a polished tray
Of soothing chocolate, or stimulating tea.

Leaving the bubbling beverage to cool,
Fresca slips softly to the needful stool, ?
Where the pathetic tale of Richardson
Eases her labour till the deed is done.
Then slipping back between the conscious sheets,
Explores a page of Gibbon as she eats. Too
Her hands caress the egg's well-rounded dome, loose Z
She sinks in revery, till the letters come.
Their scribbled contents at a glance devours,
Then to reply devotes her practic'd powers.

"My dear, how are you? I'm unwell today,
And have been, since I saw you at the play.
I hope that nothing mars your gaity,
And things go better with you, than with me.
I went last night—more out of dull despair—
To Lady Kleinwurm's party—who was there? rhyme drags it
Oh, Lady Kleinwurm's monde—no one that mattered— out to
Somebody sang, and Lady Kleinwurm chattered. diffuseness Z
What are you reading? anything that's new?
I have a clever book by Giraudoux.
Clever, I think, is all. I've much to say—
But cannot say it—that is just my way—
When shall we meet—tell me all your manoeuvers;
And all about yourself and your new lovers—
And when to Paris? I must make an end,
My dear, believe me, your devoted
friend".

trick of Pope etc
This ended, to the steaming bath she moves, not to let
Her tresses fanned by little flutt'ring Loves; couple[t] diffuse 'em
Odours, confected by the cunning French,
Disguise the good old ~~female stench~~./hearty female stench.

Carbon of typescript, of which leaves 3–5 have been renumbered 4–6 by Pound. His marginalia are in pencil.

Fresca! in other time or place had been
A meek and lowly weeping Magdalene;
More sinned against than sinning, bruised and marred,
The lazy laughing Jenny of the bard.
(The same eternal and consuming itch
Can make a martyr, or plain simple bitch);
Or prudent sly domestic puss puss cat,
Or autumn's favourite in a furnished flat,
Or strolling slattern in a tawdry gown,
A doorstep dunged by every dog in town.
For varying forms, one definition's right:
Unreal emotions, and real appetite.
Women grown intellectual grow dull,
And lose the mother wit of natural trull.
Fresca was baptised in a soapy sea
Of Symonds- Walter Pater- Vernon Lee.
The Scandinavians bemused her wits,
The Russians thrilled her to hysteric fits.
From ~~Fmxx~~such chaotic misch-masch potpourri
What are we to expect but poetry?
When restless nights distract her brain from sleep
She may as well write poetry, as count sheep.
And on those nights when Fresca lies alone,
She scribbles verse of such a gloomy tone
That cautious critics say, her style is quite her own.
Not quite an adult, and still less a child,
By fate misbred, by flattering friends beguiled,
Fresca's arrived (the Muses Nine declare)
To be a sort of can-can salonniere.
But at my back from time to time I hear
The rattle of the bones, and chuckle spread from ear to ear.

A rat crept softly through the vegetation
Dragging its slimy belly on the bank
While I was fishing in the dull canal
On a winter evening round behind the gashouse,
Musing upon the king my brother's wreck
And on the king my father's death before him.
White bodies naked on the low damp ground,
And bones cast in a little low dry garret,
Rattled by the rat's foot only, year to year.
But at my back from time to time I hear
The sound of horns and motors, which shall bring
Sweeney to Mrs.Porter in the spring.
O the moon shone bright on Mrs.Porter
And on her daghter
They wash their feet in soda water
Et O ces voix d'enfants, chantant dans la coupole!

Echo ?

Fresca! in other time or place had been
A meek and lowly weeping Magdalene;
More sinned against than sinning, bruised and marred,
The lazy laughing Jenny of the bard.
(The same eternal and consuming itch
Can make a martyr, or plain simple bitch);
Or prudent sly domestic puss puss cat,
Or autumn's favourite in a furnished flat,
Or strolling slattern in a tawdry gown,
A doorstep dunged by every dog in town.
For varying forms, one definition's right:
Unreal emotions, and real appetite.
Women grown intellectual grow dull,
And lose the mother wit of natural trull.
Fresca was baptised in a soapy sea
Of Symonds—Walter Pater—Vernon Lee.
The Scandinavians bemused her wits,
The Russians thrilled her to hysteric fits.
From ~~For~~ such chaotic misch-masch potpourri
What are we to expect but poetry?
When restless nights distract her brain from sleep
She may as well write poetry, as count sheep.
And on those nights when Fresca lies alone,
She scribbles verse of such a gloomy tone
That cautious critics say, her style is quite her own.
Not quite an adult, and still less a child,
By fate misbred, by flattering friends beguiled,
Fresca's arrived (the Muses Nine declare)
To be a sort of can-can salonniere.
But at my back from time to time I hear
The rattle of the bones, and chuckle spread from ear to ear.

A rat crept softly through the vegetation (Echt) (1)
Dragging its slimy belly on the bank
While I was fishing in the dull canal
On a winter evening round behind the gashouse,
Musing upon the king my brother's wreck
And on the king my father's death before him.
White bodies naked on the low damp ground,
And bones cast in a little low dry garret,
Rattled by the rat's foot only, year to year.
But at my back from time to time I hear
The sound of horns and motors, which shall bring ?
Sweeney to Mrs. Porter in the spring.
O the moon shone bright on Mrs. Porter
And on her daughter
They wash their feet in soda water
Et O ces voix d'enfants, chantant dans la coupole!

Twit twit twit twit twit twit twit
Tereu tereu
So rudely forc'd.
Ter

Unreal City, I have seen and see
Under the brown fog of your winter noon
Mr.Eugenides, the Smyrna merchant,
Unshaven, with a pocket full of currants
(C.i.f. London: documents at sight),
Who asked me, in ~~abominable~~ French,
To luncheon at the Cannon Street Hotel,
And perhaps a weekend at the Metropole.

Twit twit twit
Jug jug jug jug jug jug
Tereu
O swallow swallow
Ter

London, the swarming life you kill and breed,
Huddled between the concrete and the sky,
Responsive to the momentary need,
Vibrates unconscious to its formal destiny,

Knowing neither how to think, nor how to feel,
But lives in the awareness of the observing eye.
Phantasmal gnomes, burrowing in brick and stone and steel!
Some minds, aberrant from the normal equipoise
(London, your people is bound upon the wheel!)
Record the motions of these pavement toys
And trace the cryptogram that may be curled
Within these faint perceptions of the noise
Of the movement, and the lights!

Not here, O Ademantus, but in another world.

At the violet hour, the hour when eyes and back and hand
Turn upward from the desk, the human ~~engine~~ waits -
Like a taxi throbbing waiting at a stand -
~~To spring~~ to pleasure through the horn or ivory gates,

I Tiresias, though blind, throbbing between two lives,
Old man with wrinkled female breasts, can see
At the violet hour, the evening hour that strives
Homeward, and brings the sailor home from sea,

Twit twit twit twit twit twit twit
Tereu tereu
So rudely forc'd.
Ter

Unreal City, I have seen and see
Under the brown fog of your winter noon
Mr. Eugenides, the Smyrna merchant,
Unshaven, with a pocket full of currants
(C.i.f. London: documents at sight),
Who asked me, in ~~abominable~~ French,
To luncheon at the Cannon Street Hotel,
And (perhaps) a weekend at the Metropole.

vocative ?

demotic

?

Twit twit twit
Jug jug jug jug jug jug
Tereu
O swallow swallow
Ter

London, the swarming life you kill and breed,
Huddled between the concrete and the sky,
Responsive to the momentary need,
Vibrates unconscious to its formal destiny,

Knowing neither how to think, nor how to feel,
But lives in the awareness of the observing eye.
~~London, your people is bound upon the wheel~~!
(Phantasmal) gnomes, burrowing in brick and stone and steel!
Some minds, aberrant from the normal equipoise
(London, your people is bound upon the wheel!)
Record the motions of these pavement toys
And trace the cryptogram that may be curled
Within these faint perceptions of the noise
Of the movement, and the lights!

vocative ??

Not here, O Ademantus, but in another world.

At the violet hour, the hour when eyes and back and hand
Turn upward from the desk, the human ~~engine~~ waits—
Like a taxi throbbing waiting at a stand—
(~~To spring~~ to pleasure through the horn or ivory gates,)

Taxi spring ??

I Tiresias, though blind, throbbing between two lives,
Old man with wrinkled female breasts, can see
At the violet hour, the evening hour that strives
Homeward, and brings the sailor home from sea,

Line 120: Ademantus = Adeimantus.

The typist home at teatime, who ~~begins~~
~~To clear her broken breakfast~~ away her broken breakfast, lights
Her stove, and lays out squalid food ~~in tins,~~
Prepares the room and sets the room to rights.

Out of the window perilously spread
Her drying combinations meet the sun's last rays,
And on the divan piled, (at night her bed),
Are stockings, dirty camisoles, ~~and stays.~~

A bright kimono wraps her as she ~~sprawls~~
In nerveless torpor on the window seat;
A touch of art is given by the false
Japanese print, ~~purchased in Oxford Street.~~

I Tiresias, old man with wrinkled dugs,
Perceived the scene, and foretold the rest,
~~Knowing the manner of these crawling bugs,~~
I too awaited the expected guest.

~~A youth of twentyone,~~ spotted about the face,
One of those simple loiterers whom we say
We may have seen in any public place
At almost any hour of night or day.

~~Pride has not fired him with ambitious rage,~~
His hair is thick with grease, and thick with scurf,
~~Perhaps~~ his inclinations touch the stage -
~~Not sharp enough to associate with the turf.~~

He, the young man carbuncular, ~~will stare~~
~~Boldly about~~, in "London's one cafe",
And he will tell her, with a casual air,
Grandly, "I have been with Nevinson today".

Perhaps a cheap house agent's clerk, who flits
Daily, from flat to flat, with one bold stare;
One of the low on whom assurance sits
As a silk hat on a Bradford millionaire.

He munches with the same peristent stare,
He knows his way with women (and that's that!)
Impertinently tilting back his chair
And dropping cigarette ash on the mat.

The time is now propitious, as he guesses,
The meal is ended, she is bored and tired;
Endeavours to engage her in caresses,
Which still are unreproved, if undesired.

verse not interesting enough as verse to warrant so much of it.

The typist home at teatime, who ~~begins~~
~~To~~ clears ~~her broken breakfast~~ away her (broken) breakfast, lights
Her stove, and lays out squalid food ~~in tins,~~
Prepares the room and sets the room to rights.

qui dira les gaffers de la rime (1)

Out of the window perilously spread
Her drying combinations meet the sun's last rays,
And on the divan piled, (at night her bed),
Are stockings, dirty camisoles, ~~and stays.~~

inversions not warranted by any real exegience of metre

A bright kimono wraps her as she sprawls
In nerveless torpor on the (window seat;)
A touch of art is given by the false
Japanese print, ~~purchased in Oxford Street.~~

? not in that lodging house ?

I Tiresias, old man with wrinkled dugs,
Perceived the scene, and foretold the rest,
~~Knowing the manner of these crawling bugs,~~
I too awaited the expected guest.

Too easy

~~A youth of twentyone~~, spotted about the face,
One of those simple loiterers whom we say
We may have seen in any public place
At almost any hour of night or day.

Personal

~~Pride has not fired him with ambitious rage,~~
His hair is thick with grease, and thick with scurf,
Perhaps his inclinations touch the stage—
~~Not sharp enough to associate with the turf.~~

Perhaps be damned.

He's the young man carbuncular, will stare
~~Boldly about~~, in "London's one cafe",
And he will tell her, with a casual air,
Grandly, "I have been with Nevinson today".

alternate nights

~~Perhaps a cheap~~ house agent's clerk, who flits
Daily, from flat to flat, with one bold stare;
One of the low on whom assurance sits
As a silk hat on a Bradford millionaire.

He munches with the same persistent stare,
He knows his way with women (and that's that!)
Impertinently tilting back his chair
And dropping cigarette ash on the mat.

The time is now propitious, as he guesses,
The meal is ended, she is bored and tired;
Endeavours to engage her in caresses,
Which still are unreproved, if undesired.

mix up of the couplet & grishkin (2) not good—

Flushed and decided, he assaults at once,
Exploring hands encounter no defence;
His vanity requires no response,
And makes a welcome of indifference.

(And I Tiresias have foresuffered all
Enacted on this same divan or bed,
I who have sat by Thebes beneath the wall
And walked among the lowest of the dead.

[Echt]

-Bestows one final patronising kiss,
And gropes his way, finding the stairs unlit;
~~And at the corner where the stable is,~~
~~Delays only to urinate, and spit.~~] [probably over the mark]

She turns and looks a moment in the glass,
Hardly aware of her departed lover;
Across her brain one half-formed thought may pass:
"Well now that's done, and I am glad it's over".

[make up yr. mind]

When lovely woman stoops to folly and
[Paces] ~~She~~ moves about her room again, alone,
She smoothes her hair with automatic hand,
And puts a record on the gramophone.

[you Tiresias if you know know damn well or else you dont.]

"This music crept by me upon the waters"
And along the Strand, and up ~~the ghastly hill of~~ Cannon Street,
Fading at last, behind by flying feet,
There where the tower was traced against the night
Of Michael Paternoster Royal, red and white.

Flushed and decided, he assaults at once,
Exploring hands encounter no defence;
His vanity requires no response,
And makes a welcome of indifference.

(And I Tiresias have foresuffered all
Enacted on this same divan or bed,
I who have sat by Thebes beneath the wall
And walked among the lowest of the dead.

Echt

—Bestows one final patronising kiss,
And gropes his way, finding the stairs unlit;
~~And at the corner where the stable is,~~
~~Delays only to urinate, and spit~~.

probaly over the mark

She turns and looks a moment in the glass,
Hardly aware of her departed lover;
Across her brain one half-formed thought ~~may~~ pass:
"Well now that's done, and I am glad it's over".

make up yr. mind

When lovely woman stoops to folly and
Then ~~She~~ moves about her room again, alone,
She smoothes her hair with automatic hand,
And puts a record on the gramophone.

you Tiresias if you know know damn well or else you dont.

"This music crept by me upon the waters"
And along the Strand, and up ~~the ghastly hill of~~ Cannon Street,
Fading at last, behind my flying feet,
There where the tower was traced against the night
Of Michael Paternoster Royal, red and white.

The river sweats
Oil and tar
The barges drift
With the turning tide
Red sails ~~swing~~ wide
~~to~~ leeward
Swing on the heavy spar.
The barges wash
~~As~~ Drifting logs,
~~Down~~ Greenwich reach
Past the Isle of Dogs.
Weialala leia
~~[illegible] ooohhhh~~
Wallala ~~leialala~~

Elizabeth and Leicester.
Beating oars.
The ~~stern~~ was formed
~~A~~ a gilded shell.
Red and gold.
The ~~brisk~~ swell
Rippled both shores
South west wind
Carried down stream
The peal of bells.
~~There were the~~ White towers.

Weialala ~~lalalala~~ leia
Wallala leialala.

The river sweats
~~o~~/Oil and tar
The barges drift
With the turning tide
Red sails ~~swing~~ wide
to leeward
Swing On the heavy spar.
The barges wash,
~~Like~~/~~As~~ drifting logs,
~~Past~~/Down Greenwich reach
Past the Isle of Dogs.
Weialala leia
~~O O hin hein heinh~~ ~~wei~~/~~o o a hanhhh~~
Wallala ~~leialala~~

Elizabeth and Leicester.
Beating oars.
The ~~barge~~/stern was formed
~~As~~ a gilded shell~~s~~,
Red and gold.
The ~~slow~~/brisk swell
Rippled both shores
South west wind
Carried down stream
The peal of bells.
~~There are still w~~/White towers.

Weialala ~~lalalala~~ leia
~~Weialala~~/Wallala leialala.

First draft, in pencil, of lines 266–91.

Type this passage only

"Highbury bore me. Highbury's children
Played under green trees and in the dusty Park.
~~We~~ were humble people and conservative
As neither the rich nor the working class know.
My father had a small business, somewhere in the City
A small business, an anxious business, ~~which~~ providing only
The house in Highbury, and three weeks at ~~Shanklin~~ Bognor.
Highbury bore me. Richmond and Kew
Undid me. At ~~Kew we had tea.~~
~~Near Richmond on the river~~, ~~at last~~ I raised my knees
~~Stretched~~ on the floor of a perilous canoe.

or

"Trams and dusty trees.
Highbury bore me. Richmond and Kew
Undid me. ~~Beyond~~ By Richmond I raised my knees
Stretched on the floor of a perilous canoe".

5-R echt

"My feet ~~are~~ are at Moorgate, and my heart
Under my feet. After the event
He wept. He ~~offered~~ promised "a new start".
I made no ~~outcry~~ comment: what should I resent?"

Type out this anyhow

"Highbury bore me. Highbury's children
Played under green trees and in the dusty Park.
~~We~~/Mine were humble people and conservative
As neither the rich nor the working class know.
My father had a small business, somewhere in the city
A small business, an anxious business, ~~whi~~ provid~~ed~~/ing only
The house in Highbury, and three weeks at ~~Shanklin.~~ Bognor.
Highbury bore me. Richmond and Kew
Undid me. ~~At Kew we had tea.~~
= ~~At~~/~~Near Richmond on the river at last~~ I raised my knees
O.K. ~~Stretched o~~/On the floor of a perilous canoe.

"Trams and dusty trees.
O. K. Highbury bore me. Richmond and Kew
Undid me. ~~Beyond~~ By Richmond I raised my knees
echt Stretched on the floor of a perilous canoe".

"My feet ~~were~~/are at Moorgate, and my heart
Under my feet. After the event
He wept. He ~~offere~~ promised 'a new start'.
I made no ~~outery~~ comment: what shd I resent?"

First draft in pencil of lines 292–9. Pound's marginalia are in pencil and in green crayon.

"~~I went to the pictures.~~ ~~On~~ Margate Sands
~~There were many others.~~ I can connect
Nothing with nothing. ~~He had~~
I still feel the pressure of dirty hands

"~~On~~ Margate Sands.
I can connect
Nothing with nothing.
~~The~~ broken fingernails of dirty hands.
My people ~~—~~ ~~plain~~ humble people, who expect
Nothing".

la la.

To Carthage then I came.

Burning burning burning burning
O Lord thou pluckest me out
O Lord thou pluckest

burning

~~“I was to be grateful~~. On Margate sands
~~There were many others.~~ I can connect
Nothing with nothing. ~~He had~~
I still feel the pressure of dirty hand 286

113
97
“On Margate Sands. 76
I can connect
  Nothing with nothing.
The broken finger nails of dirty hands.
humble
My people ~~are~~ ~~plain~~ people, who expect
~~n~~/Nothing”.

la la

To Carthage then I came

Burning burning burning burning
O Lord thou pluckest me out
O Lord thou pluckest

burning

Verso of leaf. First pencil draft of lines 300–11. The figures on the right probably refer to the number of lines in Sections I, II, and V. Page 5 was not included in the total of Section I.

Part IV. Death by Water.

The sailor, attentive to the chart or to the sheets,
A concentrated will against the tempest and the tide,
Retains, even ashore, in public bars or streets
Something inhuman, clean and dignified.

Even the drunken ruffian who descends
Illicit backstreet stairs, to reappear,
For the derision of his sober friends,
Staggering, or limping with a comic gonorrhea,

From his trade with wind and sea and snow, as they
Are, he is, with "much seen and much endured",
Foolish, impersonal, innocent or gay,
Liking to be shaved, combed, scented, manicured.

* * * * *

"Kingfisher weather, with a light fair breeze,
Full canvas, and the eight sails drawing well.
We beat around the cape and laid our course
From the Dry Salvages to the eastern banks.
A porpoise snored upon the phosphorescent swell,
A triton rang the final warning bell
Astern, and the sea rolled, asleep.
Three knots, four knots, at dawn; at eight o'clock
And through the forenoon watch, the wind declined

Part IV. Death by Water. (1)

The sailor, attentive to the chart or to the sheets,
A concentrated will against the tempest and the tide,
Retains, even ashore, in public bars or streets
Something inhuman, clean and dignified.

Bad—but
cant attack
until I get
typescript

Even the drunken ruffian who descends
Illicit backstreet stairs, to reappear,
For the derision of his sober friends,
Staggering, or limping with a comic gonorrhea,

From his trade with wind and sea and snow, as they
Are, he is, with "much seen and much endured", (2)
Foolish, impersonal, innocent or gay,
Liking to be shaved, combed, scented, manucured.

* * * * *

"Kingfisher weather, with a light fair breeze,
Full canvas, and the eight sails drawing well.
We beat around the cape and laid our course
From the Dry Salvages to the eastern banks.
A porpoise snored upon the phosphorescent swell,
A triton rang the final warning bell
Astern, and the sea rolled, asleep.
Three knots, four knots, at dawn; at eight o'clock
And through the forenoon watch, the wind declined;

Manuscript, in black ink, on four leaves. The writing suggests that Eliot may have been copying from an unpreserved draft. Lines 1–83 are unpublished.

Line 12: manucured = manicured.

Thereafter everything went wrong.
A watercask was opened, smelt of oil,
Another brackish. Then the main gaff jaws
Jammed. A spar split for nothing, bought
And paid for as good Norwegian pine. Fished.
And then the garboard-strake began to leak.
The canned baked beans were only a putrid stench
Two men came down with gleet; one cut his hand.
The crew began to murmur; when one watch
~~Took ha~~ Was overtime at dinner, justified
Extenuated thus: "Eat!" they said,
"It aint the eating what there is to eat—
"For when you got through digging out the weevils
"From every biscuit, there's no time to eat".
So this injurious race was sullen, and kicked;
Complained too of the ship. "*Her* sail to windward
Said one of influence amongst the rest,
"I'll see a dead man in an iron coffin,
"With a crowbar now from here to Hell, before
"This vessel sail to windward".
So the crew moaned; the sea with many voices
Moaned all about us, under a rainy moon,
While the suspended winter heaved and tugged,
Stirring foul weather under the Hyades.
Then came the fish at last. The eastern ~~northern~~ ~~banks~~
Had never known the codfish run so well.

Thereafter everything went wrong.
A watercask was opened, smelt of oil,
Another brackish. Then the main gaffjaws
Jammed. A spar split for nothing, bought
And paid for as good Norwegian pine. Fished.
And then the garboard-strake began to leak.
The canned baked beans were only a putrid stench.
Two men came down with gleet; one cut his hand.
The crew began to murmur; when one watch
~~Took to~~ Was over time at dinner, justified
Extenuated thus: "Eat!" they said,
"It aint the eating what there is to eat—
"For when you got through digging out the weevils
"From every biscuit, there's no time to eat".
So this injurious race was sullen, and kicked;
Complained too of the ship. "*Her* sail to windward,"
Said one of influence amongst the rest,
"I'll see a dead man in an iron coffin,
"With a crowbar row from here to Hell, before
"This vessel sail to windward".
So the crew moaned; the sea with many voices
Moaned all about us, (1) under a rainy moon,
While the suspended winter heaved and tugged,
Stirring foul weather under the Hyades.
Then came the fish at last. The ~~northern~~ eastern ~~seas~~/banks
Had never known the codfish run so well.

So the men pulled the nets, and laughed, and thought
Of home, and dollars, and the pleasant violin
At Marm Brown's joint, and the girls and gin.
I laughed not.
For an unfamiliar gust
Laid us down. And freshened to a gale.
We lost two dories. And another night
Observed us scudding, with the trysail gone,
Northward, leaping beneath invisible stars
And when the lookout could no longer hear
Above the roar of waves upon the sea
The sharper note of breakers on a reef,
We knew we had passed the farthest northern island
So no one spoke again. We ate slept drank
Hot coffee, and kept watch, and no one dared
To look into another's face, or speak
In the horror of the illimitable scream
Of a whole world about us. One night
On watch, I thought I saw in the fore cross-trees
Three women ~~with~~ leaning forward, with white hair
Streaming behind, who sang above the wind
A song that charmed my senses, while I was
Frightened beyond fear, horrified past horror, calm,
(Nothing was real) for, I thought, now, when
I like, I can wake up and end the dream.

3

So the men pulled the nets, and laughed, and thought
Of home, and dollars, and the pleasant violin
At Marm Brown's joint, and the girls and gin.
I laughed not.
For an unfamiliar gust
Laid us down. And freshened to a gale.
We lost two dories. And another night
Observed us scudding, with the trysail gone,
Northward, leaping beneath invisible stars
And when the lookout could no longer hear
Above the roar of waves upon the sea
The sharper note of breakers on a reef,
We knew we had passed the farthest northern islands
So no one spoke again. We ate slept drank
Hot coffee, and kept watch, and no one dared
To look into anothers face, or speak
In the horror of the illimitable scream
Of a whole world about us. One night
On watch, I thought I saw in the fore cross-trees
Three women ~~with w~~ leaning forward, with white hair
Streaming behind, who sang above the wind
A song that charmed my senses, (1) while I was
Frightened beyond fear, horrified past horror, calm,
(Nothing was real) for, I thought, now, when
I like, I can wake up and end the dream.

– Something which we knew must be a dawn –
A different darkness, flowed above the clouds,
And dead ahead we saw, where sky and sea should meet,
A line, a white line, a long white line,
~~Toward which we~~ A wall, a barrier, towards which we drove.
My God man there's bears on it.
Not a chance.   Home and mother.
Where's a cocktail shaker, Ben, here's plenty of cracked ice.
Remember me.

And if Another knows, I know I know not,
Who only know that there is no more noise now.

*   *   *   *   *

Phlebas, the Phoenician, a fortnight dead,
Forgot the cry of gulls, and the deep-sea swell
And the profit and loss.
A current under sea
Picked his bones in whispers. As he rose and fell
He passed the stages of his age and youth
Entering the whirlpool.
Gentile or Jew,
O you who turn the wheel and look to windward,
Consider Phlebas, who was once handsome and tall as you.

—Something which we knew must be a dawn—
A different darkness, flowed above the clouds,
And dead ahead we saw, where sky and sea should meet,
A line, a white line, a long white line,
    A wall, a barrier,
~~Toward which we~~ towards which we drove.
My God man there's bears on it.
Not a chance. Home and mother.
Where's a cocktail shaker, Ben, (1) here's plenty of cracked ice.
Remember me.

And if <u>Another</u> knows, I know I know not,
Who only know that there is no more noise now.

* * * * *

Phlebas, the Phoenician, a fortnight dead, (2)
Forgot the cry of gulls, and the deep-sea swell
And the profit and loss.
                                        A current under sea
Picked his bones in whispers. As he rose and fell
He passed the stages of his age and youth
Entering the whirlpool.
                                        Gentile or Jew,
O you who turn the wheel and look to windward,
Consider Phlebas, who was once handsome and tall as you.

Lines 84–93 were published alone as Section IV.

DEATH BY WATER.

~~The~~

The sailor, ~~attentive to the chart and to the sheets.~~
~~A concentrated will against the tempest and the tide,~~
Retains, ~~even~~ ashore, in public bars or streets
Something inhuman, ~~clean, and~~ dignified.

~~Even the~~ drunken ~~ruffian who~~ descends
Illicit ~~backstreet~~ stairs, ^ ~~travel~~ to reappear,
For the derision of his sober friends,
Staggering, or limping with a ~~comic~~ gonnorrhea,

Yet
From his trade with wind and sea ~~and snow, as they~~
~~Are, he is, with~~ "much seen and much endured",
~~Foolish, impersonal, innocent or gay,~~
Liking to be shaved, combed, scented, manucured.

~~Kingfisher weather~~, with a light fair breeze,
~~Full canvas, and the eight sails drawing well.~~
We beat around the cape ~~and laid our course~~
From the Dry Salvages ~~to the eastern banks.~~
A porpoise snored ~~upon~~ the ~~phosphorescent~~ swell,
~~A triton rang the final warning bell~~
Astern, and the sea rolled, asleep.
Three knots, four knots, ~~at dawn; at eight o'clock~~

DEATH BY WATER.

The sailor, ~~attentive to the chart and to the sheets.~~
~~A concentrated will against the tempest and the tide,~~
Retains, ~~even~~ ashore, in public bars or streets
Something inhuman, ~~clean, and~~ dignified.

~~Even the~~ drunken ~~ruffian who~~ descends
Illicit ~~backstreet~~ stairs, thence to reappear,
For the derision of his sober friends,
Staggering, or limping with a ~~comic~~ gonnorrea,

Yet From his trade with wind and sea ~~and snow, as they~~
~~Are, he is, with~~ "much seen and much endured",
~~Foolish, impersonal, innocent or gay,~~
Liking to be shaved, combed, scented, manucured.

~~Kingfisher weather~~, with a light fair breeze,
~~Full canvas, and the eight sails drawing well.~~
We beat around the cape ~~and laid our course~~
From the Dry Salvages ~~to the eastern banks.~~
A porpoise snored ~~upon~~ the ~~phosphorescent~~ swell,
~~A triton rang the final warning bell~~
Astern, and the ~~sea rolled~~, asleep.
Three knots, four knots, ~~at dawn; at eight o'clock~~

Typescript of the manuscript, typed with the violet ribbon used by Pound. His markings are in pencil.
Line 8: gonnorrea = gonorrhea, gonorrhoea.
Line 12: manucured = manicured.

And through the forenoon watch, the wind declined;
Thereafter everything went wrong;
A water-cask was opened, smelt of oil,
Another brackish. The the main gaff jaws
Jammed. A spar split for nothing, bought
And paid for as good Norwegian pine. Fished.
And then the garboard strake began to leak.
The canned baked beans were only a putrid stench.
Two men came down with gleet; one cut his hand.
The crew began to murmur; when one watch
Was overtime at dinner, justified,
Extenuated thus: "Eat !" they said,
"It aint the eating what there is to eat,
For when you got through digging out the weevils
From every biscuit, theres no time to eat".
So this injurious race was sullen, and kicked;
Complained too of the ship. "Her sail to windward",
Said one of influence amongst the rest,
"I'll seee a dead man in an iron coffin
With a crowbar row from here to hell, before
This vessel sail to windward".
So the crew moaned, the sea with many woices
Moaned all about us, under a rainy moon,
While the suspended winter heaved and tugged,
Stirring foul weather under the Hyades.
Then came the fish at last, the northern seas
Had never known the codfish run so well.
So the men pulled the nets, and laughed, and thought
Of home and dollars and the pleasant violin
At Marm Brown's joint, and the girls and gin.

And through ~~the~~ forenoon watch, ~~the~~ wind declined;
Thereafter everything went wrong,
A water-cask ~~was~~ opened, smelt of oil,
~~Another brackish. The[n] the main gaff jaws~~
~~Jammed.~~ A spar split for nothing, bought
And paid for as good Norwegian pine. ~~Fished.~~
~~And then the~~ The garboard strake began to leak.
The canned baked beans were ~~only a putrid~~ stench.
Two men came down with gleet; ~~one cut his hand.~~
~~The crew began to murmur~~; ~~when one watch~~
Was ~~overtime at dinner~~, ~~justified~~,
~~Extenuated thus:~~ "Eat!" they said,
"It aint the eating what there is to eat,
For when you got through digging out the weevils
~~From every biscuit~~, theres no time to eat".
So this ~~injurious~~ race was sullen, and kicked;
Complained too of the ship. "Her sail to windward",
~~Said one of influence amongst the rest,~~
"I'll see a dead man in an iron coffin
With a crowbar row from here to hell, before
This vessel sail to windward".
~~So the crew moaned~~, the sea with many voices
Moaned all about us, under a rainy moon,
While the suspended winter heaved and tugged,
Stirring foul weather under the Hyades.
Then came the fish at last, ~~the northern seas~~
Had never known the codfish run so well.
So the men pulled the nets, and laughed, and thought
Of home and dollars and the pleasant violin
At Marm Brown's joint, and the girls and gin.

I laughed not.
                                        For an unfamiliar gust
Laid us down.   And freshened to a gale.
We lost two dories.   And another night
Observed us scudding, with the trysail gone,
Northward, leaping beneath invisible stars.
And when the lookout could no longer hear
Above the roar of waves upon hthe sea
The sharper note of breakers on a reef,
We knew we had passed the farthest northern islands,
So no one spoke again.   We ate slept drank
Hot coffee, and kept watch, and no one dared
To look into anothers face, or speak
In the horror of the illimitable scream
Of a whole world about us."   One night
On watch, I thought I saw in the fore cross trees
Three women leaning forward, with white hair
Streaming behind, who sang above the wind
A song that charmed my senses, while I was
Frightened beyond fear, horrified past horror, calm.
(Nothing was real)   for, I thought, now, when
I like, I can wake up and end the dream,

Something which we knew must be a dawn-
A different darkness, flowed above the clouds,
And dead ahead we saw, where sky and sea should meet,
A line, a white line, a long white line,
A wall, a barrier, towards which we drove.

3.

I laughed not.
                    For an unfamiliar gust
Laid us down. And freshened to a gale.
We lost two dories. And another night
Observed us scudding, with the trysail gone,
Northward, leaping beneath invisible stars.
And when the lookout could no longer hear
Above the roar of waves upon the sea
The sharper note of breakers on a reef,
We knew we had passed the farthest northern islands,
So no one spoke again. We ate slept drank
Hot coffee, and kept watch, and no one dared
To look into anothers face, or speak
In the horror of the illimitable scream
Of a whole world about us. One night
On watch, I thought I saw in the fore cross trees
Three women ~~with white hair~~ leaning forward, with white hair
Streaming behind, who sang above the wind
A song that charmed my senses, while I was
Frightened beyond fear, horrified past horror, calm.
(Nothing was real) for, I thought, now, when
I like, I can wake up and end the dream.

Something which we knew must be a dawn—
A different darkness, flowed above the clouds,
And dead ahead we saw, where sky and sea should meet,
A line, a white line, a long white line,
A wall, a barrier, towards which we drove.

My God man theres bears on it.

Not a chance, Home and nother.

Wheres a cocktail shaker, Ben, heres plenty of cracked ice.

And if Another knows, I know I know not,

Who only k ow that there is no more noise now.

PPhlebas the Phoenician, a fortnight dead,

Forgot the cry of gulls, and the deep sea swell

And the profit and loss.

A current under sea

Picked his bones in whispers. As he rose and fell

He passed the stages of his age and youth

Enteri g the whirlpool.

Gentile or Jew,

O you who turn the wheel and look to windward,

Consider Phlebas, who was once handsome and tall as you.

4

My God man theres bears on it.
Not a chance.   Home and mother.
Wheres a cocktail shaker, Ben, heres plenty of cracked ice.

And if Another knows, I know I know not,
Who only know that there is no more noise now.

Phlebas the Phoenician, a fortnight dead,
Forgot the cry of gulls, and the deep sea swell
And the profit and loss.
                                        A current under sea
Picked his bones in whispers. As he rose and fell
He passed the stages of his age and youth
Entering the whirlpool.
                                        Gentile or Jew,
O you who turn the wheel and look to windward,
Consider Phlebas, who was once handsome and tall as you.

Line 81 of the manuscript, 'Remember me.', has been omitted from this copy.

OK from here on I think.

After the torchlight red on sweaty faces
After the frosty silence in the gardens
After the agony in stony places
The shouting and the crying
~~Gardens~~ Prisons and palaces and reverberation
Of thunder of spring ~~of~~ over ~~the~~ distant mountains
He who was living is now dead
We who were living are now dying
With a little patience

Here is no water but only rock
Rock and no water and the sandy road
The road winding ~~ahead~~ above among the mountains
Which are mountains of rock without water
If there were water we should stop and drink
Amongst the rock one cannot stop or think
The sweat is dry and the feet ~~cannot stop~~ are in the sand
If there were only water amongst the rock
Dead mountain mouth ~~with~~ of ~~carious~~ rotten teeth that cannot spit
Here one can neither stand nor lie nor sit
There is not even silence in the mountains
But dry sterile thunder and no rain
There is not even solitude in the mountains
But red sullen faces sneer and snarl
From doors of mudcracked houses

OK   OK from
here on
I think.

After the torchlight red on sweaty faces (1)
After the frosty silence in the gardens
After the agony in stony places
The shouting and the crying
Prisons
~~Gardens~~ and palaces and reverberation
distant
Of thunder of spring ~~of~~ over ~~the~~ mountains
He who was living is now dead,
We who were living are now dying
With a little patience

Here is no water but only rock (2)
Rock and no water and the sandy road
above
The road winding ~~ahead~~ among the mountains
Which are mountains of rock without water
If there were water we should stop and drink
Amongst the rock one cannot stop or think
are in the sand
The sweat is dry and the feet ~~cannot stop~~
st
~~st~~
If there were only water among the rock
of rotten
Dead mountain mouth ~~with~~ ~~carious~~ teeth that cannot spit
Here one can neither stand nor lie nor sit
There is not even silence in the mountains
But dry sterile thunder and no rain
There is not even solitude in these mountains
But red sullen faces sneer and snarl
From doors of mudcracked houses

First draft, in pencil, on six leaves, untitled, of 'What the Thunder Said'. Pound's comment is in green crayon and in ink.

If there were water
And no rock
If there were rock
And also water
And water
A spring
A pool among the rock
If there were the sound of water only
Not the cicada, and
~~Dead~~ Dry grass singing
But sound of water over a rock
Where the hermit thrush sings in the pine trees
Drip-drop drip drop drop drop-drop
But ~~there~~ is no water

Who is the third that walks always beside~~s~~ you?
When I count, there is only you and I together
But when I look ahead up the white road
There is always another one walking beside you
Gliding wrapt in a brown mantle, hooded
I do not know whether a man or a woman
- But who is that on the other side of you?

What is that sound high in the air
Murmur of maternal lamentation
Who are those hooded hordes swarming

2

If there were water
And no rock
If there were rock
And also water
And water
A spring
A pool among the rock
If there were the sound of water only
Not the cicada, and
~~The d~~/Dry grass singing
                                        a
But sound of water over^rock
                                        sings
Where the hermit thrush in the pines/trees
            drip-drop
Drip-drop^drop drop drop
But ~~here~~/there is no water

                                    always
Who is the third that walks^besides you?
When I count, there is only you and I together
But when I look ahead up the white road
                                one   ~~there~~
There is always another^walking^beside you
Gliding wrapt in a brown mantle, hooded
                                                    a
I do not know whether a man or^woman
—But who is that on the other side of you?

What is that sound high in the air
Murmur of maternal lamentation
Who are those hooded hordes swarming

Over ~~Polish~~ endless plains, stumbling in cracked earth
Ringed with a flat horizon only.
What is the city over the mountains
Cracks and reforms and ~~breaks~~ bursts in the violet air
Falling towers
Jerusalem, Athens, Alexandria
Vienna, London. ~~Unreal~~
Unreal

A woman drew her long black hair out tight
And fiddled whisper music on those strings
And bats with baby faces, in the violet ~~air~~ light,
Whistled, and beat their wings
A ~~form~~ crawled downward down a blackened wall
And upside down in air were towers
Tolling reminiscent bells, that kept the hours.
And voices singing out of empty cisterns and
exhausted wells.

~~The infant hydrocephalous, who sat~~
~~By a bridge end, by a dried-up water course~~
~~And fiddled (with a knot tied in one string)~~

~~We [illegible]~~

~~perished~~
endless
Over ~~Polish~~ plains, stumbling in cracked earth
Ringed with a flat horizon, only.
What is the city over the mountains
bursts
Cracks and reforms and breaks in the violet air
Falling
~~Tumbling~~ towers
~~Athens~~/Jerusalem, Athens, Alexandria
Vienna, London. ~~Unreal~~
Unreal

A woman drew her long black hair out tight
And fiddled whisper music on those strings
And bats with baby faces, in the violet ~~air~~ light,
Whistled, and beat their wings
A ~~man~~/form crawled downward down a blackened wall
And upside down in air were towers
Tolling reminiscent bells, that kept the hours.
And voices singing out of empty cisterns and
exhausted wells.

~~The infant hydrocephalous, who sat~~
~~By/At a bridge end, by a dried-up water course~~
~~And fiddled (with a knot tied in one string)~~

~~We come~~

Lines 65–8 are unpublished.

In this decayed hole among the mountains
In the faint moonlight, ~~the~~ grass is singing
Over the tumbled graves, about the chapel
There is the empty chapel, only the wind's home,
~~The~~ It has no windows, and the door swings,
Dry bones can harm no one.
Only a black cock stood on the rooftree
Co co rico co co rico
In a flash of lightning. Then a damp gust
Bringing rain . . .

Ganga was sunken, and the limp leaves
~~Waited~~ Waited for ~~the~~ rain, while the black clouds
Gathered far distant, over Himavant.
The jungle crouched, humped in silence.
Then spoke the thunder
DA
DATTA. ~~we [illegible]~~, what have we given?
My friend, my ~~friend~~ blood ~~[illegible]~~ shaking ~~[illegible]~~ my heart,
The awful daring of a moment's surrender
Which an age of prudence ~~cannot~~ never retract—
By this, and this only, we have existed,
Which is not to be found in our obituaries
Nor in ~~[illegible]~~ memories draped by the beneficent spider
Nor ~~in~~ under ~~documents~~ seals ~~eaten~~ broken by the lean solicitor
In our empty rooms.

In this decayed hole among the mountains
In the faint moonlight, the grass is singing
Over the tumbled graves, about the Chapel,
There is the empty chapel, only the wind's home,
It has
~~There are~~ no windows, and the door~~s~~ swing~~;~~/s,
Dry bones can harm no one.
Only, a black cock stood on the rooftree
Co co rico Co co rico
In a flash of lightning, then a damp gust
Bringing rain . . .

Ganga was sunken, and the limp leaves
Waited
~~Writhed~~ for ~~the~~ rain, while the black clouds
Gathered far distant, over Himavant.
The jungle crouched, humped in silence.
Then spoke the thunder
DA
DATTA. ~~we brother~~, what have we given?
blood shaking ~~within~~
My friend, my ~~blood~~/~~friend, beating~~ ~~in~~ my heart,
The awful daring of a moment's surrender
never
Which an age of prudence can~~not~~ retract—
By this, and this only, we have existed,
Which is not to be found in our obituar~~y~~/ies,
~~industrious~~
draped ~~shrouded~~ by ~~kindly~~
~~those treasures over which creeps the~~
~~that~~
Nor in memories ~~which will busy beneficent~~,^spiders~~s~~
the beneficent
under seals broken
Nor ~~in~~ ~~documents~~ ~~eaten~~ by the lean solicitor
In our empty rooms.

Line 85: 'we brother': very doubtful reading.

DA.

Dayadhvam. ~~friend, my friend~~ I have heard the
Turn in the door, once and once only
We think of the key, each in his prison,
Thinking of the key, each confirms a prison
Only at nightfall, aethereal ~~murmurs~~ rumours
~~Restore the for a moment~~ [Revive ~~the spirits~~ of] a broken Coriolanus.

DA

Damyata. ~~The wind was fair, and~~ the boat respon
Gaily, to the hand expert with sail and ~~wheel~~ oar.
The sea was calm, ~~and~~ your [would have] heart responded
Gaily, when invited, beating ~~responsive~~ [obedient]
To controlling hands. ~~I left without you~~
~~Clasping empty hands~~ I sat upon the shore
Fishing, with ~~the desolate sunset~~ [the arid plain] behind me
~~Which is not of the land~~ Shall I at least set ~~the~~ [my] lands in order

5

DA.
Dayadhvam. ~~friend, my friend~~ I have heard the key
Turn in the door, once and once only.
We think of the key, each in his prison,
Thinking of the key, each ~~has built~~/confirms a prison.
rumours
Only at nightfall, aetherial ~~murmurs~~
Revive ~~the spirits~~ of
~~Repair/Restore the for a moment~~ a broken Coriolanus,
for a moment
DA
Damyata. ~~the wind was fair, and~~ the boat responded
~~rudder.~~
Gaily, to the hand expert with sail and ~~wheel.~~
oar.
would have
The sea was calm, ~~and~~ your heart responded
obedient
Gaily, when invited, beating ~~responsive~~
~~You over on the shore~~
To controlling hands. ~~I left without you~~
~~There I leave you~~
~~Clasping empty hands~~ I ~~sit~~/sat upon ~~the~~/a shore
the arid plain
Fishing, with ~~the/a desolate sunset~~ behind me
~~Can~~/Shall I at least set my ~~own~~ lands~~-~~
~~Which now at last my/the kingdom~~ in order?

London Bridge is falling down falling down falling

Poi s'ascose nel foco che gli affina.
Quando fiam ceu chelidon – O swallow swallow
~~Why then Ile fit you. Hieronymo's mad againe.~~
Le prince d'Aquitaine de la tour abolie.
These fragments I have spelt shored against into my ruins.
Why then Ile fit you. Hieronymo's mad againe.
~~Datta. Dayadhvam, Damyata.~~
Datta. Dayadhwam. damyata.

Shantih Shantih Shantih.

London Bridge is falling down falling down falling down

Poi s'ascose nel fuoco che gli affina.
  Quando fiam ceu chelidon—O swallow swallow.
~~Why then Ile fit you. Hieronimo's mad againe.~~
Le prince d'Aquitaine de la tour abolie
                    shored against
These fragments I have spelt into my ruins. (1)
  Why then Ile fit you. Hieronimo's mad againe.
~~Datta, dayadhvam, damyata.~~
  Datta. Dayadhvam, damyata.

        Shantih shantih shantih.

Line 111: nel fuoco] nel foco.
Line 113: de la tour] à la tour.
Between lines 112–13, and line 115 Hieronimo's] Hieronymo's.

WHAT THE THUNDER SAID.

After the torchlight red on sweaty faces,
After the frosty silence in the gardens,
After the agony in stony places,
The shouting and the crying,
Prison and palace and reverberation
Of thunder of spring over distant mountains;
He was living is now dead,
We who were living are now dying
With a little patience

Here is no water but only rock
Rock and no water and the sandy road
The road winding above among the mountains
Which are mountains of rock without water
If there were water we should stop and drink
Amongst the rock one cannot stop or think
The sweat is dry and the feet are in the sand
If there were only water amongst the rock
Dead mountain mouth of carious teeth that cannot spit
Here one can neither stand or lie or sit
There is not even silence xxxxx in the mountains
But dry sterile thunder without rain
There is not even solitude in the mountains
But red sullen faces sneer and snarl
From doors of mudcracked houses

If there were water

And no rock
If there were rock
And also water

WHAT THE THUNDER SAID.

After the torchlight red on sweaty faces,
After the frosty silence in the gardens,
After the agony in stony places,
The shouting and the crying,
Prison and palace and reverberation
Of thunder of spring over distant mountains;
He who was living is now dead,
We who were living are now dying
With a little patience

Here is no water but only rock
Rock and no water and the sandy road
The road winding above among the mountains
Which are mountains of rock without water
If there were water we should stop and drink
Amongst the rock one cannot stop or think
The sweat is dry and the feet are in the sand
If there were only water amongst the rock
Dead mountain mouth of carious teeth that cannot spit
Here one can neither stand [n]or lie [n]or sit
There is not even silence ~~among~~ in the mountains
But dry sterile thunder without rain
There is not even solitude in the mountains
But red sullen faces sneer and snarl
From doors of mudcracked houses

If there were water
And no rock
If there were rock
And also water

Typescript of the manuscript. In violet ink on the double foolscap used by Pound, it may have been typed by him, or by Eliot when he visited his friend in Paris on his way home from Lausanne, where this section was written.

And water
A spring
A pool among the rock
If there were the sound of water only
Not the cicada
And dry grass singing
But sound of water over a rock
Where the hermit thrush sings in the pine trees
Drip drop drip drop drop drop drop
But there is no water

Who is the third who walks always beside you?
When I count, there is only you and I together
But when I look ahead up the white road
There is always another one walking beside you
Gliding wrapt in a brown mantle, hooded
I do not know whether a man or a woman
-But who is that on the other side of you?

What is that sound high in the air
Murmur of maternal lamentation
Who are those hooded hordes swarming
Over endless plains, stumbling in cracked earth
Ringed by the flat horizon only
What is the city over the mountains
Cracks and reforms and bursts in the violet air
Falling towers
Jerusalem Athens Alexandria
Vienna London
Unreal

A woman drew her long black hair out tight
And fiddled whisper music on those strings

And water
A spring
A pool among the rock
If there were the sound of water only
Not the cicada
And dry grass singing
But sound of water over a rock
Where the hermit thrush sings in the pine trees
Drip drop drip drop drop drop drop
But there is no water

Who is the third who walks always beside you?
(it) (are)
When I count, there is only you and I together
But when I look ahead up the white road
There is always another one walking beside you
Gliding wrapt in a brown mantle, hooded
I do not know whether a man or a woman
—But who is that on the other side of you?

What is that sound high in the air
Murmur of maternal lamentation
Who are those hooded hordes swarming
Over endless plains, stumbling in cracked earth
Ringed by the flat horizon only
What is the city over the mountains
Cracks and reforms and bursts in the violet air
Falling towers
Jerusalem Athens Alexandria
Vienna London
Unreal

A woman drew her long black hair out tight
And fiddled whisper music on those strings

And bats with baby faces, in the violet light
Whistled, and beat their wings
A form crawled downward down a blackened wall
And upside down in air were towers
Tolling reminiscent bells, that kept the hours
And voices singing out of empty cisterns and exhausted wells.

In this decayed hole among the mountains
In the faint moonlight, the grass is singing
Over the tumbled graves, about the chapel
There is the empty chapel, only the wind's home,
It has no windows, and the door swings,
Dry bones can harm no one.
Only a black cock stood on the roof tree.
Co co rico co co rico
In a flash of lightning.   Then a damp gust
Bringing rain

Ganga was sunken, and the limp leaves
Waited for rain, while the black clouds
Gathered far distant, over Himavant.
The jungle crouched, humped in silence.
Then spoke the thunder
DA
Datta: what have we given?
My friend, blood shaking my heart,
The awful daring of a moment's surrender
Which an age of prudence can never retract
By this, and this only, we have existed,
Which is not to be found in our obituaries
Or in memories draped by the beneficent spider
Or under seals broken by the lean solicitor
In our empty rooms.

And bats with baby faces, in the violet light
Whistled, and beat their wings
~~A form~~ And crawled head downward down a blackened wall
And upside down in air were towers
Tolling reminiscent bells, that kept the hours
And voices singing out of empty cisterns and exhausted wells.

In this decayed hole among the mountains
In the faint moonlight, the grass is singing
Over the tumbled graves, about the chapel
There is the empty chapel, only the wind's home,
It has no windows, and the door swings,
Dry bones can harm no one.
Only a black cock stood on the roof trees
Co co rico co co rico
In a flash of lightning. Then a damp gust
Bringing rain

Ganga was sunken, and the limp leaves
Waited for rain, while the black clouds
Gathered far distant, over Himavant.
The jungle crouched, humped in silence."
Then spoke the thunder
  DA
Datta: what have we given?
My friend, blood shaking my heart,
The awful daring of a moment's surrender
Which an age of prudence can never retract
By this, and this only, we have existed,
Which is not to be found in our obituaries
Or in memories draped by the beneficent spider
Or under seals broken by the lean solicitor
In our empty rooms.

DA

Dayadhvam: I have heard the key
Turn in the door once and turn once only
We think of the key, each in his prison
Thinking of the key, each confirms a prison
Only at nightfall, aetherial rumours
Revive for a moment a broken Coriolanus.

DA

Damyata: The boat responded
Gaily, to the hand expert with sail and oar
The sea was calm, your heart would have responded
Gaily, when invited, beating obedient
To controlling hands.

I sat upon the shore
Fishing, with the arid plain behind me
Shall I at least set my lands in order?

London Bridge is falling down, falling down, falling down

Poi s'ascose nel fuoco che gli affina
Quando fiam ceu chelidon - O swallow swallow
Le Prince d'Aquitaine de la tour abolie
These fragments I have shored against my ruins
Why then Ile fit you. Hieronymo's mad againe.
Datta. Dayadhvam. Damyata.

Shantih shantih shantih

DA
Dayadhvam: I have heard the key
Turn in the door once and turn once only
We think of the key, each in his prison
Thinking of the key, each confirms a prison
Only at nightfall, aetherial rumours
Revive for a moment a broken Coriolanus.
DA
Damyata: The boat responded
Gaily, to the hand expert with sail and oar
The sea was calm, your heart would have responded
Gaily, when invited, beating obedient
To controlling hands.
                                        I sat upon the shore
Fishing, with the arid plain behind me
Shall I at least set my lands in order?

London Bridge is falling down, falling down, falling down

Poi s'ascose nel fuoco che gli affina
Quando fiam ceu chelidon—O swallow swallow
Le Prince d'Aquitaine de la tour abolie
These fragments I have shored against my ruins
Why then Ile fit you. Hieronymo's mad againe.
Datta. Dayadhvam. Damyata.

            Shantih   shantih   shantih

Line 107: nel fuoco] nel foco.
Line 109: de la tour] à la tour.

Come under the shadow of this grey rock
Come ~~in under~~ under the shadow of this grey rock
And I will show you a shadow different from either
Your shadow sprawling over the sand at daybreak, or
Your shadow huddled by the fire against the red rock.
I will show you his bloody cloth and ~~queer~~ bloodless limbs
And the ~~blue~~ grey shadow between his lips.

He walked first between the sea and the high cliffs
When the wind made him aware of his legs smoothly passing each other
~~and his knees grasping each other~~
And of his arms crossed over his breast.
When he walked over the meadows
He was stifled and carried apart
By the river
His eyes were aware of the pointed corners of his eyes
And his hands were aware of long fingers.
So because he was struck ~~mad~~ dumb by the knowledge of his own be
He could not live men's ways, but became a dancer to God.
If he walked in city streets, in the streets of Carthage
He seemed to tread on ~~pale~~ faces, convulsive ~~thighs and~~ knees
So he came out to live under the rock.

First he wished that he had been a tree
To push its branches among each other.

Come under the shadow of this grey rock
Come (~~and sit~~) under the shadow of this grey rock
And I will show you a shadow different from either
Your shadow sprawling over the sand at daybreak, or
Your shadow huddled by the fire against the redrock.
cloth ~~bloodless~~
I will show you his bloody ~~cloth~~/coat and ~~green~~ limbs
grey
And the ~~blue~~ shadow between his lips.

He walked first between the sea and the high cliffs
smoothly
Where the wind made him aware of his legs passing each other
~~and his knees grasping each other~~
And of his arms crossed over his breast.
When he walked over the meadows
He was stifled and carried apart
By the river
His eyes were aware of the pointed corners of his eyes
And his hands were aware of long fingers.
down
So because he was struck mad by the knowledge of his own beauty
He could not live mens' ways, but became a dancer to God.
If he walked in city streets, in the streets of Carthage
~~many~~ thighs and
He seemed to tread on ~~pale~~ faces, convulsive ~~thighs~~ knees.
So he came out to live under the rock.

First he wished that he had been a tree
To push its branches among each other.

First draft, untitled, in pencil, recto and verso, of 'The Death of St. Narcissus'. The leaf is torn and creased. The first five lines, revised (see fair copy also, p. 95), became lines 26–9 of 'The Waste Land'.

And taught its roots among each other

Then he wished that he had been a fish
With slippery white belly ~~caught~~ held between his own fingers
To have writhed in his own clutch, his beauty
caught in ~~[illegible]~~ of his own beauty

Then he wished he had been a young girl
Caught in the woods by a drunken old man
To have known at the last moment, the full
taste of her own whiteness
The horror of her own smoothness.

[illegible] to God.
Because his flesh was in love with the penetrant arrow
He danced on the hot sand
Until the arrows came.
He surrendered himself and embraced them
And his whiteness and redness satisfied him.
~~We can have the kind of life we want, but his~~
~~life went straight to the death he wanted.~~

Now he is ~~green~~ dry and stained
With the shadow in his mouth.

~~a~~/And tangle its roots among each other

Then he wished that he had been a fish
held
With slippery white belly ~~caught~~ between his own fingers
To have writhed in his own clutch, his beauty
 caught in ~~the net of~~ his own beauty

Then he wished he had been a young girl
Caught in the woods by a drunken old man
To have known at the last moment, the full
 taste of her own whiteness
  The horror of her own smoothness.

So he devoted himself to God.
Because his flesh was in love with the penetrant arrows
He danced on the hot sand
Until the arrows came.
He surrendered himself and embraced them
And his whiteness and redness satisfied him.
~~We each have the sort of life we want, but his~~
 ~~life went straight to the death he wanted.~~

Now he is ~~green~~ dry and stained
With the shadow in his mouth.

Line 31: 'devoted himself': uncertain reading.

The death of Saint Narcissus.

Come under the shadow of this grey rock
Come in under the shadow of this grey rock
And I will show you a shadow different from either
Your shadow sprawling over the sand at daybreak, or
Your shadow leaping ~~by~~ behind the fire against the red rock:
I will show you his bloody cloth and limbs
And the grey shadow on his lips.

He walked once between the sea and the high cliffs
When the wind made him aware of his legs smoothly
passing each other
And of his arms crossed over his breast.
When he walked over the meadows
He was stifled and soothed by his own rhythm.
By the river
His eyes were aware of the pointed corners of his eyes
And his hands aware of the tips of his fingers.
Struck down by such knowledge
He could not live men's ways, but became a dancer before Go
If he walked in city streets
He seemed to tread on faces, ~~convulsed~~ convulsive thighs and knees.
So he came out to live under the rock.

P.T.O.

The death of ~~a~~ Saint Narcissus. (1)

Come under the shadow of this grey rock
Come in under the shadow of this grey rock
And I will show you a shadow different from either
Your shadow sprawling over the sand at daybreak, or
Your shadow leaping ~~by~~ behind the fire against the red rock:
I will show you his bloody cloth and limbs
And the grey shadow on his lips.

He walked once between the sea and the high cliffs
Where the wind made him aware of his legs smoothly passing each other
And of his arms crossed over his breast.
When he walked over the meadows
He was stifled and soothed by his own rhythm.
By the river
His eyes were aware of the pointed corners of his eyes
And his hands aware of the tips of his fingers.
Struck down by such knowledge
He could not live mens' ways, but became a dancer before God.
If he walked in city streets
He seemed to tread on faces, convuls~~ed~~ive thighs and knees.
So he came out to live under the rock.

P.T.O.

Fair copy, in black ink, on both sides of the leaf. Published, with variants, in *Poems Written in Early Youth* (1950), from the text of the *Poetry* galley proof.

First he was sure that he had been a tree
Twisting its branches among each other
And tangling its roots among each other.

Then he knew that he had been a fish
With slippery white belly held tight in his own fingers,
Writhing in his own clutch, his ancient beauty
Caught fast in the pink tips of his new beauty.

Then he had been a young girl
Caught in the woods by a drunken old man
Knowing at the end the taste of her own whiteness
The horror of her own smoothness,
And he felt drunken and old.

So he became a dancer to God.
Because his flesh was in love with the burning arrow
He danced on the hot sand
Until the arrows came.
As he embraced them his white skin surrendered
itself to the redness of blood, and satisfied him.
Now he is green, dry and stained
With the shadow in his mouth.

First he was sure that he had been a tree
Twisting its branches among each other
And tangling its roots among each other.

Then he knew that he had been a fish
With slippery white belly held tight in his own fingers,
Writhing in his own clutch, his ancient beauty
Caught fast in the pink tips of his new beauty.

Then he had been a young girl
Caught in the woods by a drunken old man
Knowing at the end the taste of her own whiteness
The horror of her own smoothness,
And he felt drunken and old.

So he became a dancer to God.
Because his flesh was in love with the burning arrows
He danced on the hot sand
Until the arrows came.
As he embraced them his white skin surrendered
  itself to the redness of blood, and satisfied him.
Now he is green, dry and stained
With the shadow in his mouth.

SONG ~~FOR THE OPHELIA~~

The golden foot I may not kiss or clutch
Glowed in the shadow of the bed
~~Perhaps it does not come to very much~~
This thought this ghost this pendulum in the head
Swinging from life to death
Bleeding between two lives

Waiting ~~that~~ a touch ~~that~~ a breath

The wind sprang up and broke the bells
Is it a dream or something else
When the surface of the blackened river
Is a face that sweats with tears?
I saw across ~~the sullen~~ river
The campfires shake the spears

~~Waiting that touch~~

~~[illegible]~~

SONG. ~~FOR THE OPHERION.~~ (1)

georgian

The golden foot I may not kiss or clutch
Glowed in the shadow of the bed
~~Perhaps it does not come to very much~~
This thought this ghost this pendulum in the head
Swinging from life to death
Bleeding between two lives

Waiting ~~that~~ a touch ~~that~~ a breath

The wind sprang up and broke the bells
Is it a dream or something else
When the surface of the blackened river
Is a face that sweats with tears?

I saw across ~~the~~ a ~~sullen~~ river — an alien?
The campfires shake the spears

~~Waiting that touch~~

~~After thirty years.~~

Typescript, revised in pencil, with Pound's markings in pencil and in ink. Published pseudonymously as 'Song to the Opherian' in *The Tyro* (April 1921), lines 8–13 were also used (with changes) in 'The wind sprang up at four o'clock'.

EXEQUY.

Persistent lovers will repair
(In time) to my suburban tomb,
A pilgrimage, when I become
A local deity of love,
  And pious vows and votive prayer
Shall hover in my sacred grove
  Sustained on that Italian air.

When my athletic marble form
Forever gracious, ever young,
With grateful garlands shall be hung
And flowers of deflowered maids
  The constant flame shall keep me warm,
A bloodless shade among the shades
  Doing no good, but not much harm.

While the melodious fountain falls
(Carved by the cunning Bolognese)
The Adepts twine beneath the trees
The sacramental exercise.
  They terminate the festivals
  With some invariable surprise
  Of fireworks, of an Austrian walz.

But if, more violent, more profound,
One soul, disdainful or disdained,
Shall come, his shadowed beauty stained
The colour of the withered year,
  Self-immolating on the Mound
Lost at the crisis, he shall hear
  A breathless chuckle underground.
SOVEGNA VOS AL TEMPS DE MON DOLOR.

EXEQUY. (1)

Persistent lovers will repair
(In time) to my suburban tomb,
A pilgrimage, when I become
A local deity of love,
  And pious vows and votive prayer
Shall hover in my sacred grove
  Sustained on that Italian air.

When my athletic marble form
Forever lithe, forever ~~Forever gracious, ever~~ young,
With grateful garlands shall be hung
And flowers of deflowered maids;
  The [~~constant~~] cordial flame shall keep me warm, cordial
A bloodless shade among the shades O.K.
  Doing no good, but not much harm.
nor yet

While the melodious [fountain] falls
(Carved by the cunning Bolognese)
The Adepts/twine beneath the trees [in
~~The sacramental~~ exercise. sacrificial In sacramental
  They terminate the festivals
  With [~~some~~] an invariable surprise This is Laforgue
  Of fireworks, or an Austrian waltz. not XVIII
  The

But if, more violent, more profound,
One soul, disdainful or disdained,
~~Shall~~ come, his shadowed beauty stained
with [The] colour of [the] colours withered year,
  Self-immolating on the Mound
Upon [~~Just at~~] the crisis, [~~he shall~~] hear
  A breathless chuckle underground.
~~SOVEGNA VOS AL TEMPS DE MON DOLOR~~. (2)
~~Consiros vei la pasada folor~~. (3)
S

ꟼ (——) at the c [risis] hear

Typescript, with pencilled revisions, and Pound's marginalia in pencil and in ink. Unpublished.
Line 29: AL TEMPS DE MON DOLOR = A TEMPS DE MA DOLOR
la pasada = la passada.

Pride sobered, in the clinging mire

~~Where the mystic waters falls~~

~~The adepts sipped in 28 baths~~

~~In conduits led the waters [illegible]~~ the lines

~~The scattered [illegible]~~

~~Down ornamental terraces~~

The smooth mel. waters fall

Where are adepts nothing

Pudibund, in the clinging vine (1)
~~Where the m. waters fall~~

mystics
The ~~adepts~~/~~votaries~~ grouped in twos and threes
adepts

~~In conduits led between~~ the trees
Are scattered underneath
~~Down ornamental terraces~~
The smooth mel. waters fall
Where am. adepts recline

Verso of leaf. Rough pencil draft, apparently of an alternative third stanza for 'Exequy'; m. and mel. for melodious; am. for amorous. Line 3: 'grouped': uncertain reading. These lines are numbered consecutively for reference, but the numbering does not indicate the order in which they were written.

THE DEATH OF THE DUCHESS.

I

The inhabitants of Hampstead have silk hats
On Sunday afternoon go out to tea
On Saturday have tennis on the lawn, and tea
On Monday to the city, and then tea.
They know what they are to feels and what to think,
They know it with the morning printer's ink
They have another Sunday ~~when the last is gone~~
They know what to think and what to feel
The inhabitants of Hampstead are bound forever on the wheel.

But what is there for you and me
For me and you
What is there for us to do?
Where the leaves meet in leafy Marylebone?

~~In hampstead there is nothing new~~
~~And in the evening, through lace curtains, the aspidestra grieves.~~

II

In the evening people hang upon the bridge rail
Like onions under the eaves.
In the square they lean against each other, like sheaves
Or walk like fingers on a table
Dogs ~~heads~~ eyes reaching over the table
Are their heads when they stare
Supposing that they have the heads of birds
Beaks and no words,

What words have we?

I should like to be in a crowd of beaks without words
But it is terrible to be alone with another person.

We should have marble floors
And firelight on your hair
There will be no footsteps up and down the stair

The people leaning against another in the square
Discuss the evening's news, and other bird things.

My thoughts tonight have tails, but no wings.
They hang in clusters on the chandelier
Or drop one by one upon the floor.
Under the brush her hair
Spread out in little fiery points of will
Glowed ~~like~~ words, then was suddenly still.

"You have into cause to love me, I did enter you in my heart
Before ever you vouvhsafeed to ask for the key".

THE DEATH OF THE DUCHESS.

I

The inhabitants of Hampstead have silk hats
On Sunday afternoon go out to tea
On Saturday have tennis on the lawn, and tea
On Monday to the city, and then tea.
They know what they are to feel and what to think,
They know it with the morning printer's ink
They have another Sunday ~~when the last is gone~~
They know what to think and what to feel
The inhabitants of Hampstead are bound forever on the wheel.

But what is there for you and me
For me and you
What is there for us to do ?
Where the leaves meet in leafy Marylebone?

~~In Hampstead there is nothing new~~
~~And in the evening, through lace curtains, the aspidestra grieves.~~

II

II In the evening people hang upon the bridge rail
Like onions under the eaves.
In the square they lean against each other, (1) like sheaves
Or walk like fingers on a table
Dogs ~~heads~~ eyes reaching over the table
Are in their heads when they stare
Supposing that they have the heads of birds
Beaks and no words,

? (What words have we?)

I should like to be in a crowd of beaks without words
But it is terrible to be alone with another person.

We should have marble floors
And firelight on your hair
There will be no footsteps up and down the stair

The people leaning against another in the square
Discuss the evening's news, and other bird things.

My thoughts tonight have tails, but no wings.
They hang in clusters on the chandelier
Or drop one by one upon the floor.
Under the brush her hair
Spread out in little fiery points of will
Glowed ~~like~~ into words, then was suddenly still.

"You have cause to love me, I did enter you in my heart
Before ever you vouchsafed to ask for the key". (2)

* ~~anticipate~~?

Typescript, on two leaves, with the title added in black ink. Pound's marginalia are in pencil. Unpublished.
Lines 35–7, revised, became lines 108–10 of 'The Waste Land'.
Line 15: aspidestra = aspidistra.
* anticipate?: very doubtful reading.

With her back turned, her arms were bare
Fixed for a question, her hands behind her hair
And the firelight shining where the muscle drew.

My thoughts in a tangled bunch of heads and tails —
One suddenly released, fell to the floor
One that I knew:
"Time to regain the door".
It crossed the carpet and expired on the floor.

And if I said "I love you" should we breathe
Hear music, go a-hunting, as before?
The hands relax, and the brush proceed?
Tomorrow when we open to the chambermaid
When we open the door
Could we address her or should we be afraid?
If it is terrible alone, it is sordid with one more.

If I said "I do not love you" we should breathe
The hands relax, and the brush proceed?
How terrible that it should be the same!
In the morning, when they knock upon the door
We should say: This and this is what we need
And if it rains, the closed carriage at four.
We should play a game of chess
The ivory men make company between us
We should play a game of chess
Pressing lidless eyes and waiting for a knock upon the door.

Time to regain the door.

"When I grow old, I shall have all the court
Powder their hair with arras, to be like me.
But I know you love me, it must be that you love me".

Then I suppose they found her
As she turned
To interrogate the silence fixed behind her.

~~I am steward of her revenue~~
~~But I know, and I know she knew~~..

×

With her back turned, her arms were bare
Fixed for a question, her hands behind her hair
And the firelight shining where the muscle drew.

My thoughts in a tangled bunch of heads and tails —
One suddenly released, fell to the floor
One that I knew:
Pruf [rock] "Time to regain the door". (1)
It crossed the carpet and expired on the floor.

And if I said "I love you" should we breathe) cadence
Hear music, go a-hunting, (2) as before? reproduction
The hands relax, and the brush proceed? from Pr [ufrock]
Tomorrow when we open to the chambermaid or Por [trait
When we open the door of a Lady]
Could we address her or should we be afraid?
If it is terrible alone, it is sordid with one more.

If I said "I do not love you" we should breathe
The hands relax, and the brush proceed?
rhythm ? How terrible that it should be the same!
In the morning, when they knock upon the door
We should say: This and this is what we need ~~?? particularize~~
And if it rains, the closed carriage at four.
We should play a game of chess
The ivory men make company between us
We should play a game of chess
Pressing lidless eyes and waiting for a knock upon the door.

Time to regain the door.

"When I grow old, I shall have all the court (3)
Powder their hair with arras, to be like me.
But I know you love me, it must be that you love me".

Then I suppose they found her (4)
As she turned ~~(?)~~
To interrogate the silence fixed behind her.

(~~I am steward of her revenue~~
~~But I know, and I know she knew . . .~~)

Lines 60–1 and 64 became lines 136–8 of 'The Waste Land'. On the verso Eliot has pencilled:

Encounter
—
Imprisonment
Flight Meeting
Afterwards

These words may refer to the plot of *The Duchess of Malfi*.

Indecipherable cancellation by Pound between lines 68–9.

After the turning of ~~a thousand~~ The inspired days
After the praying [~~and the crying~~] and the silence and the crying
And the inevitable ending of a thousand ways
And frosty vigil kept ~~in the~~ withered gardens
After the life and death of lonely places
After the judges and the advocates and wardens
And the torchlight red on sweaty faces
After the turning of inspired nights
And the shaking spears and flickering lights –
After the living and the dying –

After the ending of this inspiration
And the torches and the faces and the shouting
The world seemed petite –
The ~~world was ended~~ – like a Sunday outing.

the inspired
After the turning of ~~a thousand~~ days (1)
After the praying (~~and crying~~) and the silence and the ~~sighing~~/crying
And the inevitable ending of a thousand ways

kept
And frosty vigil ^ in ~~the~~ withered gardens
After the life and death of lonely places
After the judges and the advocates and wardens
And the torchlight red on sweaty faces
After the turning of inspired nights
the
And shaking spears and flickering lights—
After the living and the dying—

After the ending of this inspiration
And the torches and the faces and the shouting
{ The world seemed futile—
~~show~~
{ ~~The world was ended~~—like a Sunday outing.

First draft, untitled, in black ink. Unpublished. Line 7 became, with the substitution of 'After' for 'And', line 322 of 'The Waste Land'.

I am the Resurrection and the Life
I am the things that stay, and those that flow.
I am the husband and the wife
And the victim and the sacrificial knife
I am the fire, and the butter also.

I am the Resurrection and the Life (I)
I am the things that stay, and those that flow.
I am the husband and the wife
And the victim and the sacrificial knife
I am the fire, and the butter also.

Fair copy (?), untitled, in black ink. Unpublished.

So through the evening, through the violet air

~~One~~ Some ~~tortured~~ tortured meditation dragged me on [be]

Concatenated words {wherefrom / from which / whereof} the sense {had / seemed gone / was}

– When comes, to the sleeping or the wake

The This-do-ye-for-my-sake

[When] To the sullen sunbaked houses and the [withered] trees

The ^one essential word ~~which~~ that frees

The inspiration ~~which~~ that delivers and expresses

~~[Illegible]~~ This wrinkled ~~withered~~ road ~~that~~ which twists and ^winds and guesses:

Oh, through the violet sky, through the evening air

A chain of reasoning ~~of which~~ whereof the thread was ~~lost~~ gone

Gathered strange images through which {we walked alone: / I walked along}

A woman drew her long black hair out tight

And fiddled whisper-music on those strings

The shrill bats quivered through the violet air

~~Sobbing~~ Whining, and beating wings.

A man, ~~[illegible]~~ distorted / contorted by some mental blight

Yet of abnormal powers

{Such a one crept / I saw him creep head downward down a wall

And upside down in air were towers

Tolling reminiscent bells –

And [there were] chanting voices out of cisterns and of wells.

My feverish {impulses / impulsions} gathered head.

A man lay flat upon his back, and ~~cried~~

"It seems that I have been a long time dead:

Do not report me to the established world[be]

{~~The world~~ It has seen ~~strange~~ {revolutions / Catalepsies} since ~~I died~~".

It has seen strange revolutions; {~~I decide~~ / let me hide".

So through the evening, through the violet air
~~Some~~ led
One ~~A/Some~~ tortured meditation dragged me on
wherefrom / had
Concatenated words { from which the sense { seemed gone—
whereof / was
—When comes, to the sleeping or the wake
The This-do-ye-for-my-sake
[When] To the sullen sunbaked houses and the [~~withered~~] trees
one essential ~~which~~ that
The^word ~~that~~ frees
that
The inspiration ~~which~~ delivers and expresses
~~withered~~ which winds and
~~[When] To the~~/This wrinkled^road ~~that~~ twists and^guesses:
~~withered~~
Oh, through the violet sky, through the evening air
whereof
A chain of reasoning ~~of which~~ the thread was ~~lost~~ gone
I
Gathered strange images through which { we walked { alone:
along

A woman drew her long black hair out tight (1)
And fiddled whisper-music on those strings
The Shrill bats quivered through the violet air
~~Sobbing~~ Whining, and beating wings.
distorted
A man, ~~one withered~~ by some mental blight
contorted
Yet of abnormal powers
{ Such a one crept
{ I saw him creep head downward down a wall
And upside down in air were towers
Tolling reminiscent bells—
And [there were] chanting voices out of cisterns and of wells.
impulses
My feverish { impulsions gathered head
A man lay flat upon his back, and ~~said~~/cried
"It seems that I have been a long time dead:
Do not report me to the established world"
It
{ ~~The world~~ has seen strange { revolutions since I died".
catalepsies
I abide
It has seen strange { revolutions: { let me bide".

First draft, untitled, in black ink, on both sides of the leaf. Five lines at the bottom of the page, a few words, and the arrow, are in pencil. Lines 13–16 and 19–22 were adapted as lines 377–84 of 'The Waste Land'.

~~Like~~ As a ~~blind man~~ deaf mute swimming deep below the surface
Knowing neither up nor down, Swims down and down
In the calm deep water where no stir ~~nor surface~~ nor surf is
Swims down and down;
And about his hair the seaweed purple and brown.

So more fixed confusion we persisted, at from town.

As deaf mute
~~Like~~ a ~~blind man~~ swimming deep below the surface
Knowing neither up nor down, swims down and down

nor surf is
In the calm deep water where no stir ~~nor surface~~
Swims down and down;
And about his hair the seaweed purple and brown.

So in our fixed confusion we persisted, out from town.

Verso of leaf. Line 28: 'blind man' cancelled, and 'deaf mute' added, in pencil.

Elegy

Our prayers dismiss the parting shade
And breathe ~~the~~ the hypocrite's amen!
The wronged Aspatia returned
Breathed in the mingled cyclamen.

How steadfastly I should have mourned
The sinking of so dear a head!
Were't not for dreams: ~~a~~ a dream restores
The ~~very~~ always inconvenient dead.

The sweat transpired from my pores!
I saw sepulchral gates, ~~flung~~ wide,
Reveal (as in a tale by Poe)
The features of the injured bride!

That hand, prophetic and slow
(Once warm, once lovely, often kissed)
Tore the disordered cerements,
Around that head the scorpions hissed!

Remorse unbounded, grief intense
Had striven to expiate the fault –
But ~~interfere~~ prison not ~~with~~ ~~our~~ present bliss!
And keep within thy charnel vault!

God, in a rolling ball of fire
Pursues by day my errant feet.
~~The~~ His flames of ~~anger~~ ~~passion~~ and ~~fire~~ desire
Approach me with consuming heat.

Elegy

Our prayers dismiss the parting shade
And breathe ~~the~~/a hypocrite's amen!
—The wrong'd Aspatia (1) returned
Wreathed in the wingèd cyclamen. (2)

How steadfastly I should have mourned
The sinking of so dear a head!
~~But~~/Were't not for dreams: ~~the~~/a dream restores
        always
The ~~very~~ inconvenient dead.

The sweat transpirèd from my pores!
I saw ~~the~~/sepulchral gates, ~~thrown~~/flung wide,
Reveal (as in a tale by Poe)
The features of the injured bride!

That hand, prophetical and slow
(Once warm, once lovely, often kissed)
Tore the disordered cerements,
Around that head the scorpions hissed!

Remorse unbounded, grief intense
Had striven to expiate the fault—
                                    present
        poison   ~~nightly~~
But ~~interfere~~ not ~~with~~ ~~my~~ ^ bliss!
And keep within thy charnel vault!

God, in a rolling ball of fire
Pursues by day my errant feet.
                        ~~horror~~   desire
                          anger
~~The~~ His flames of ~~pity~~ and ~~of ire~~
                        ~~passion~~
~~a~~/Approach me with consuming heat.

First draft, in pencil. Unpublished.

Dirge.

Full fathom five your Bleistein lies
Under the flatfish and the squids.
Graves' Disease in a dead jew's eyes!
When the crabs have ~~nibbl~~ eat the lids.
Lower than the wharf rats dive
Though he suffer a sea-change
Still expensive rich and strange

That is lace that was his nose
See upon his back he lies
(Bones peep through the ragged toes)
With a stare of dull surprise
Flood tide and ebb tide
Roll ~~Stir~~ him gently side to side
See the lips unfold unfold
From the teeth, ~~bone~~ ~~yellow~~ gold in gold
~~Sea-nymphs~~ Lobsters hourly keep close watch
Hark! now I hear them scratch scratch scratch

Dirge. (1)

Full fathom five your Bleistein (2) lies
Under the flatfish and the squids.

Graves' Disease (3) in a dead {man's / jew's} eyes!
Where the crabs have ~~nibb~~ eat the lids.
Lower than the wharf rats dive
  Though he suffer~~s~~ a sea change
  Still expensive rich and strange

That is lace that was his nose
See upon his back he lies
(Bones peep through the ragged toes)
With a ~~lo~~/stare of dull surprise
Flood tide and ebb tide
Roll ~~Stir~~ him gently side to side
See the lips unfold unfold
gold in
From the teeth, ~~black~~ ~~yellow and~~ gold.
  Lobsters hourly keep ~~the~~/close
~~Sea nymphs nightly wai/tend his~~ watch
Hark now I hear them scratch scratch scratch

On verso of 'Elegy'. First draft, in pencil. Unpublished.
Line 16: ~~wai/tend his~~: very doubtful reading.

??
doubtful

Dirge.

Full fathom five your Bleistein lies
Under the flatfish and the squids.
Graves' Disease in a dead jew's eyes!
When the crabs have eat the lids.
Lower than the wharf rats dive
Though he suffer a sea-change
Still expensive rich and strange

That is lace that was his nose
See upon his back he lies
(Bones peep through the ragged toes)
With a stare of dull surprise
Flood tide and ebb tide
Roll him gently side to side
See the lips unfold unfold
From the teeth, gold in gold
Lobsters hourly keep close watch
Hark! now I hear them scratch scratch scrat

Dirge. ?? doubtful

Full fathom five your Bleistein lies
Under the flatfish and the squids.
Graves' Disease in a dead jew's eyes!
  When the crabs have eat the lids.
    Lower than the wharf rats dive
      Though he suffer a sea-change
      Still expensive rich and strange

That is lace that was his nose
  See upon his back he lies
(Bones peep through the ragged toes)
  With a stare of dull surprise
    Flood tide and ebb tide
    Roll him gently side to side
    See the lips unfold unfold
    From the teeth, gold in gold
Lobsters hourly keep close watch
Hark! now I hear them   scratch   scratch   scratch

Fair copy, in black ink.

Those are pearls that were his eyes, L
And the crab ~~shelters in~~ clambers ~~through~~ his stomach, the e
grows
And the torn algae drift above him, ~~[illegible]~~
And the sea colander.
Still & quiet brother are you still and quiet

Those are pearls that were his eyes. See!
And the crab ~~shelters in~~ his stomach, the eel
clambers through grows ~~fat~~/big
And the torn algae drift above him, ~~purple, red,~~
And the sea colander.
Still and quiet brother are you still and quiet (1)

First draft, in pencil, untitled. The first line became line 48 of 'The Waste Land', with 'Look!' substituted for 'See!'

EDITORIAL NOTES

(Abbreviation: TWLC = *The Waste Land* correspondence. This refers to the three letters, two of them written by Pound, exchanged by him and Eliot between 24 December 1921 and early January 1922. They were published in *The Letters of Ezra Pound*, edited by D. D. Paige, 1950.)

Page 3. Epigraph

1. *Heart of Darkness* by Joseph Conrad.

   Pound: 'I doubt if Conrad is weighty enough to stand the citation.'

   Eliot: 'Do you mean not use the Conrad quote or simply not put Conrad's name to it? It is much the most appropriate I can find, and somewhat elucidative.'

   Pound: 'Do as you like about Conrad; who am I to grudge him his laurel crown?' (TWLC)

   The passage was omitted.

THE BURIAL OF THE DEAD

Page 5

1. *Our Mutual Friend* by Charles Dickens, chapter xvi, 'Minders and Reminders'.

   Sloppy is a foundling adopted by old Betty Higden, a poor widow. '"I do love a newspaper" she says. "You mightn't think it, but Sloppy is a beautiful reader of a newspaper. He do the Police in different voices."'

   (Eliot drew on this novel again for one of his *Practical Cats*. 'The Rum Tum Tugger' who

   '. . . will do
   As he do do'

   is a deliberate echo of Podsnap in Book I, chapter xi.)

2. 'Harrigan' from the musical play *Fifty Miles from Boston* (1907) by George M. Cohan, American composer and comic actor:

   . . . Proud of all the Irish blood that's in me
   Divil a man can say a word agin me . . .

3. Eliot has adapted lines from two songs: 'Meet me pretty Lindy by the watermelon vine' (from *By the Watermelon Vine*, words and music by Thomas S. Allen, 1904), and 'Meet me in the shade of the old apple tree, Ee-vah, I-vah, Oh-vah, Ev-a-line!' (from *My Evaline*, by Mae Anwerda Sloane, 1901).

4. On page 550 of Connorton's *Tobacco Brand Directory of the United States for 1899*, Bengal Lights are listed as both cigarettes and cheroots.

5. From *The Cubanola Glide* (words by Vincent Bryan, music by Harry von Tilzer, 1909):

   . . . Tease, squeeze, lovin' and wooin'
   Oh babe, what are you doin'? . . .

6. When Eliot was an undergraduate at Harvard, he attended melodrama at the Grand Opera House in Washington Street, Boston, and after a performance he would visit the Opera Exchange (as he recalled it in later life, although that name cannot be traced in records of the period) for a drink. The bartender, incidentally, was one of the prototypes of Sweeney.

7. Words by Hamilton Aïdé, music by Stephen Adams:

   . . . Do not forget me! Do not forget me!
   Think sometimes of me still,
   When the morn breaks, and the throstle awakes,
   Remember the maid of the mill! . . .

8. Eliot may have used a pseudonym when *Song to the Opherian* (see page 99) was published in Wyndham Lewis's magazine because there were two signed articles in the same number, but his choice of 'Gus Krutzsch' is interesting. In *The Sewanee Review* (vol. lxxiv, No. 1, Special Issue, Winter 1966), Mr. Francis Noel Lees traces the influence of Petronius' *Satyricon* on *The Waste Land*, and observes that 'Gus Krutzsch' is 'remarkably reminiscent of the English of "Encolpius", namely "the Crutch, or Crotch"'. Professor J. P. Sullivan writes that the name of Encolpius 'like most of the other names in the Satyricon, has point . . . and a Peacockian translation might be Mr. Encrotch, an appropriate choice for the protagonist of a predominantly sexual story' (*The 'Satyricon' of Petronius*, 1968).

9. George Meredith (1828–1909) was the grandson of a remarkable Portsmouth tailor whom he depicted in his novel *Evan Harrington*.

   When Eliot's father died in 1919, he wrote to his mother: 'I wanted you more for my sake than yours—to sing the Little Tailor to me. . . .' Perhaps the childhood memory of the song his father sang to him prompted the reference.

Page 7

1. Writing in the *Partisan Review* (vol. xxi, No. 2, 1954), Mr. G. L. K. Morris drew attention to similarities

between parts of *The Waste Land* and the reminiscences of Countess Marie Larisch, *My Past* (London, 1913). The assumption was that Eliot must have read the book, but in fact he had met the author (when and where is not known), and his description of the sledding, for example, was taken verbatim from a conversation he had with this niece and confidante of the Austrian Empress Elizabeth.

2. Pound is not certain, but he thinks he may have been referring to Tennyson's *Mariana*. It is definitely not a reference to Miss Marianne Moore.

Page 9

1. The Revelation of St. John the Divine 22:8.

2. J(ames) J(oyce). This line reminded Pound of *Ulysses*, but Eliot's Notes direct the reader to *Inferno*, iv. 25–7.

3. This is a general, not a specific reference to Blake, and by starting to write 'old', Pound may have had 'fashioned' in mind.

A GAME OF CHESS

Page 11

1. The cancelled title refers to the passage from the *Satyricon* of Petronius which replaced that from *Heart of Darkness* as the epigraph to *The Waste Land*:

   Nam Sibyllam quidem Cumis ego ipse oculis meis vidi in ampulla pendere, et cum illi pueri dicerent: *Σίβυλλα τί θέλεις*; respondebat illa: *ἀποθανεῖν θέλω*.

   I saw with my own eyes the Sybil at Cumae hanging in a cage, and when the boys said to her: 'Sybil, what do you want?' she answered: 'I want to die.'

2. Eliot offered these revised lines:

   Glowed on the marble where the glass
   Sustained by standards wrought with fruited vines
   Wherefrom . . .

   'O.K.' replied Pound (TWLC). However, Eliot restored *Held up* to the second line, and *Wherefrom* appeared in *The Criterion* only, all later printings reverting to *From Which*.

3. *La Nuit Blanche* by Rudyard Kipling.
   'Me and one wee Blood Red Mouse.' The poem itself has no relevance to *The Waste Land*; Pound said he was merely teasing Eliot about 'one'.

4. There is too much of the (iambic) pentameter, too regular a measure.

5. Implying (together with 'photo' on page 13) too realistic a reproduction of an actual conversation.

6. Thomas Lovell Beddoes (1803–49). The line recalled *Death's Jest-Book* to Pound, but in his Notes Eliot refers to 'Is the wind in that door still?' from *The Devil's Law-Case* by John Webster. Some years later, Eliot admitted that the source was of no significance as his adaptation of the phrase gave it a different meaning.

   . . . Curious, is it not, that Mr. Eliot
   has not given more time to Mr. Beddoes
   (T. L.) prince of morticians. . . .
   Pound: *Canto* lxxx.

7. Reviewing 'Georgian Poetry, 1916–1917' (*Lettres Anglaises*) in the *Mercure de France* (No. 476, Tome cxxvi, 16 April 1918), Henry-D Davray wrote: '. . . ces jeunes gens sont maîtres dans l'art d'écrire avant d'avoir vécu. Aussi cherchent-ils des sentiments pour les accommoder à leur vocabulaire et non des mots pour exprimer leur passion et leurs idées. . . .'

Page 13

1. An allusion to Paolo and Francesca, who are in the second circle of Hell, which contains the souls of the lustful. *Inferno*, v. 73–5:

   '. . . volontieri
   parlerei a que' duo, che insieme vanno,
   e paion sì al vento esser leggieri.'

   'Willingly would I speak with those two that go together, and seem so light upon the wind' (Temple Classics).

   In his misery, the protagonist of 'A Game of Chess' remembers the moment of ecstasy in the hyacinth garden; Francesca recounting her sad story to Dante, says:

   'Nessun maggior dolore,
   che ricordarsi del tempo felice
   nella miseria . . .'
   Inferno, v. 121–3

   'There is no greater pain than to recall a happy time in wretchedness.'

2. Molly Bloom's soliloquy in the Penelope episode of *Ulysses* begins and ends with 'Yes', described gaily by Joyce as 'the most positive word in the human language'.

3. 'O.K.' wrote Pound when Eliot suggested as an alternative: 'A closed car. I can't use taxi more than once' (TWLC).

4. This line was omitted at Vivien Eliot's request. The author restored it, from memory, when he made a fair copy of the poem for the sale in aid of the London Library in June 1960.

5. Eliot said this passage was 'pure Ellen Kellond', a maid employed by the Eliots, who recounted it to them.

THE FIRE SERMON

Page 23

1. This opening passage was written in imitation of *The Rape of the Lock*.

   Cf. also the Calypso episode in Joyce's *Ulysses*.

   Pound '. . . induced me to destroy what I thought an excellent set of couplets;' wrote Eliot of his pastiche, 'for, said he, "Pope has done this so well that you cannot do it better; and if you mean this as a burlesque, you had better suppress it, for you cannot parody Pope unless you can write better verse than Pope—and you can't"' (Introduction to *Selected Poems* of Ezra Pound, 1928). Eliot added, in the *Paris Review* (1959), that Pound advised him to '"Do something different"'.

2. Fresca is first mentioned in *Gerontion* (1920):

   . . . De Bailhache, Fresca, Mrs. Cammel, whirled
   Beyond the circuit of the shuddering Bear
   In fractured atoms. . . .

   Eliot: 'Do you advise printing *Gerontion* as a prelude in book or pamphlet form?'

   Pound: 'I do *not* advise printing *Gerontion* as preface. One don't miss it *at* all as the thing now stands. To be more lucid still, let me say that I advise you NOT to print *Gerontion* as prelude.' (TWLC)

3. Vivien Eliot contributed an article, 'Letters of the Moment—II', over the initials FM (pseudonym Fanny Marlow), to *The Criterion* (vol. 2, No. 7, 1924), in which these lines occur:

   When sniffing Chloe, with the toast and tea,
   Drags back the curtains to disclose the day,
   The amorous Fresca stretches, yawns, and gapes,
   Aroused from dreams of love in curious shapes.
   The quill lies ready at her finger tips;
   She drinks, and pens a letter while she sips:
   'I'm very well, my dear, and how are you?
   I have another book by Giraudoux.
   My dear, I missed you last night at the Play;

   Were you not there? Or did you slip away?
   Or were you in the seats of cheaper price?
   Dorilant sat with me, and I looked nice.
   Once settled in my box, he never stirred—
   I told him you were there, but I don't think he heard. . . .'

   Her hands caress the egg's well-rounded dome;
   As her mind labours till the phrases come.

   But see, where Fresca in her boudoir sits,
   Surrounded by a court of sparkish wits:
   Her practised eye directs its conscious darts
   At the small tyrants of the several Arts. . . .

   It probably amused Eliot to print 'these few poor verses' knowing that only two other people knew their source. In addition he drafted (pencil holograph in a black exercise book) the two paragraphs that follow, ending with a parody of *Prufrock*: '. . . if one had said, yawning and settling a shawl, "O no, I did not like the *Sacre* at all, not at all."'

4. Samuel Richardson (1689–1761). 'The pathetic tale' may have been his novel *Clarissa Harlow*.

Page 27

1. *King Lear*, III. ii. 59.

2. *Jenny*, by Dante Gabriel Rossetti.

   Lazy laughing languid Jenny
   Fond of a kiss and fond of a guinea . . .

3. John Addington Symonds (1840–93).
   Walter Horatio Pater (1839–94).
   Vernon Lee was the pseudonym of Violet Paget (1856–1935).

   These critics of the Renaissance, the source of Fresca's 'culture', are satirically linked together as aesthetes.

4. Probably the vulgar exhibitionism of the dance is implied in *can-can*, with an element of the gossip too; while *salonnière* suggests a frequenter or holder of salons, someone who moves in fashionable circles.

Page 29

1. An ironic contrast to '. . . the wonder of our age', Fulke Greville's tribute to Sir Philip Sidney.

2. The well-known boxing peers were the eighth Marquis of Queensberry (1844–1900), who supervised the drafting of the 'Queensberry rules', and the fifth Earl of Lonsdale (1857–1944), a notable boxer who donated the Lonsdale belt.

3. Virgil, *Aeneid* I. 405:

   . . . et vera incessu patuit dea.

   'and by her graceful walk, the queen of love is known'. Dryden.

Page 31

1. Palmer Cox (1840–1924) worked in America as an illustrator and author of children's books. His popular 'Brownie' series portrayed in verse and pictures the activities of a group of benevolent elves.

2. Adeimantus and Glaucon, brothers of Plato, were two of the interlocutors in *The Republic*. Appalled by his vision of the 'Unreal City', Eliot may be

alluding to the passage (Book IX. 592 A–B) which inspired the idea of the City of God among Stoics and Christians, and found its finest exponent in St. Augustine:

> *Μανθάνω, ἔφη· ἐν ᾗ νῦν διήλθομεν*
> *οἰκίζοντες πόλει λέγεις, τῇ ἐν λόγοις κειμένῃ,*
> b *ἐπεὶ γῆς γε οὐδαμοῦ οἶμαι αὐτὴν εἶναι. Ἀλλ', ἦν*
> *δ' ἐγώ, ἐν οὐρανῷ ἴσως παράδειγμα ἀνάκειται τῷ*
> *βουλομένῳ ὁρᾶν καὶ ὁρῶντι ἑαυτὸν κατοικίζειν·*

'"I understand," he [Glaucon] said: "you mean the city whose establishment we have described, the city whose home is in the ideal; for I think that it can be found nowhere on earth." "Well," said I [Socrates], "perhaps there is a pattern of it laid up in heaven for him who wishes to contemplate it and so beholding to constitute himself its citizen. . . ."' (Loeb.)

3. *Aeneid*, 6. 893–6:

> Sunt geminae Somni portae; quarum altera fertur
> cornea, qua veris facilis datur exitus umbris,
> altera candenti perfecta nitens elephanto,
> sed falsa ad caelum mittunt insomnia Manes.

> 'Two gates the silent house of Sleep adorn;
> Of polished ivory this, that of transparent horn
> True visions through transparent horn arise;
> Through polished ivory pass deluding lies.'
> Dryden.

(Cf. also *Odyssey*, 19. 559 ff.)

Eliot refers in other poems to each kind of sleep:

> And Sweeney guards the hornèd gate.
> (*Sweeney Among the Nightingales*, 1919.)

> The empty forms between the ivory gates.
> (*Ash Wednesday*, 1930.)

Page 33

1. The Café Royal. A favourite London rendezvous of writers and artists.
2. C. R. W. Nevinson, A.R.A. (1889–1946). The painter was an habitué of the Café Royal.

Page 35

1. This Wren church by Upper Thames Street was one of those listed in the *Proposed Demolition of Nineteen London Churches* (see Eliot's note to line 264). He visited them all while working in the City.

Page 41

1. Defined by Pound as 'veritable, real'.

Page 45

1. *Art Poétique* by Paul Verlaine.
   l. 25: O qui dira les torts de la Rime?
2. See *Whispers of Immortality*:

> . . . Grishkin is nice: her Russian eye
> Is underlined for emphasis;
> Uncorseted, her friendly bust
> Gives promise of pneumatic bliss.

> The couched Brazilian jaguar
> Compels the scampering marmoset
> With subtle effluence of cat;
> Grishkin has a maisonnette . . .

Pound wrote (*Canto* lxxvii):

> . . . Grishkin's photo refound years after
> with the feeling that Mr. Eliot may have
> missed something, after all, in composing his vignette
> periplum . . .

DEATH BY WATER

Page 55

1. Lines 1–84 were 'rather inspired' by the Ulysses Canto (xxvi)—'a well-told seaman's yarn'—of the *Inferno*, which ends (133–42):

> n'apparve una montagna bruna
> per la distanza, e parvemi alta tanto
> quanto veduta non n'aveva alcuna.
> Noi ci allegrammo, e tosto tornò in pianto,
> chè dalla nuova terra un turbo nacque,
> e percosse del legno il primo canto.
> Tre volte il fe' girar con tutte l'acque,
> alla quarta levar la poppa in suso,
> e la prora ire in giù, com' altrui piacque,
> infin che il mar fu sopra noi richiuso.

there appeared a mountain brown in the distance; and it seemed to me the highest that I had ever seen. We rejoiced, but soon our joy was turned to lamentation: for a storm came up from the new land, and caught the stem of our ship. Three times it whirled her round with all the waters; the fourth time it heaved up the stern and drove her down at the head, as pleased Another; until the sea closed over us.

In placing his voyage and shipwreck off the New England coast where he had sailed in his youth, Eliot makes the first mention of The Dry Salvages. Apart from Homeric overtones, his account was influenced by Tennyson's *Ulysses*, and in his essays on *Dante* (1929) and *In Memoriam* (1936) he compares Dante's and Tennyson's narrative gift: 'Dante is telling a story. Tennyson is only stating an elegiac mood.'

2. An allusion to the *Odyssey*, 1. 3–4:

> *πολλῶν δ' ἀνθρώπων ἴδεν ἄστεα καὶ νόον ἔγνω,*
> *πολλὰ δ' ὅ γ' ἐν πόντῳ πάθεν ἄλγεα ὃν κατὰ θυμόν*

> 'He saw the cities and knew the thoughts of many men
> And suffered many sorrows in his heart upon the sea.'

And also to *Ulysses*:

l. 13 'Much have I seen and known'
ll. 7–8 '. . . all times I have enjoyed
Greatly, have suffered greatly'

Page 57

1. Cf.

. . . the deep
Moans round with many voices
(*Ulysses*)

The sea has many voices
(*The Dry Salvages*)

Earlier on the same page (line 27) Eliot has written:

And then the garboard-strake began to leak.

In *Marina* (1930) line 28, he wrote:

The garboard strake leaks

Page 59

1. Sirens. Their description recalls the singing mermaids of *The Love Song of J. Alfred Prufrock*:

. . . riding seaward on the waves
Combing the white hair of the waves blown back
When the wind blows the water white and black.

Page 61

1. Ben is an obsolete nickname for a sailor.
2. Depressed by Pound's reaction to the main passage, Eliot wrote: 'Perhaps better omit Phlebas also???' 'I DO advise keeping Phlebas' replied Pound. 'In fact I more'n advise. Phlebas is an integral part of the poem; the card pack introduces him, the drowned phoen. sailor. And he is needed ABSOlootly where he is. Must stay in.' (TWLC)

WHAT THE THUNDER SAID

Page 71

1. Eliot said that he was describing his own experience of writing this section in Lausanne when he wrote in *The 'Pensées' of Pascal* (1931): '. . . it is a commonplace that some forms of illness are extremely favourable, not only to religious illumination, but to artistic and literary composition. A piece of writing meditated, apparently without progress for months or years, may suddenly take shape and word; and in this state long passages may be produced which require little or no retouch.'

   'It gives me very great pleasure to know that you like *The Waste Land*, and especially Part V. which in my opinion is not only the best part, but the only part that justifies the whole, at all' (Eliot to Bertrand Russell, 15 October 1923).
2. On 14 August 1923 Eliot wrote to Ford Madox Ford: 'There are *I* think about 30 *good* lines in *The Waste Land*. Can you find them? The rest is ephemeral.'

   'As for the lines I mention,' continued Eliot (4 October 1923) 'you need not scratch your head over them. They are the 29 lines of the water-dripping song in the last part.'

Page 81

1. On 19 May 1948 Mr. Peter Russell wrote to Eliot about the first line of Pound's *Canto* viii: 'These fragments you have shelved (shored).' Eliot replied (27 May): 'I have no idea whether Canto viii followed or preceded *The Waste Land*. I am under the impression that it followed, [it did] because of course Mr. Pound saw the manuscript of *The Waste Land* immediately on its completion and my lines certainly occurred in the draft which he saw in, I think, the month of January 1922. While I made some revisions and chiefly a great many excisions as a result of Pound's criticism of this draft, the final section of the poem remained exactly as I first wrote it. I should think also that his putting the word "shored" in brackets at the end would indicate a deliberate reference to *The Waste Land* which the reader was intended to appreciate.'

Page 95

1. Eliot could not remember when he wrote this poem, but it may have been early in 1915. In August of that year, Pound submitted it to *Poetry*; it was set up in type, though never published, and the cancelled galley-proof is now in the Harriet Monroe Collection of the University of Chicago. Variants from the present manuscript:

l. 1 grey] gray
l. 2 grey] gray
l. 3 a shadow different] something different
l. 7 grey] gray
l. 9 Where the wind] When the wind
legs] limbs
l. 15 of the tips] the pointed tips
l. 17 mens'] men's
l. 20 out to live under] out under
l. 25 *his*] his
l. 30 her own whiteness] his own whiteness
l. 31 her own smoothness] his own smoothness
No indention] Lines 8, 21, 24, 28, 33 indented.

Page 99

1. Pound: 'The song has only two lines which you can use in the body of the poem.'

   Eliot: 'Would you advise working sweats with tears etc. into nerves monologue; only place where it can go?'

   Pound: 'I dare say the sweats with tears will wait.' (TWLC)

There is no such word as 'Opherian', and it is possible that Eliot meant 'Orpharion' (from Orpheus and Arion), 'an instrument of the cittern family . . . essentially the poor man's lute' (Grove's *Dictionary of Music and Musicians*, 1954).

See also Editorial Note (8) for page 5.

Page 101

1. Discouraging Eliot from including this poem in *The Waste Land*, Pound wrote: '. . . even the sovegna doesn't hold with the rest.' (TWLC)

2. *Purgatorio*, xxvi. 147:

   be mindful in due time of my pain.

3. *Purgatorio*, xxvi. 143:

   in thought I see my past madness.

Page 103

1. 'I find that I have only one (torn) pair of pajamas, and my dictionary does not give the word for them' wrote Eliot from Marburg to Conrad Aiken (19 July 1914). 'Que faire? The dictionary, however, gives the German equivalents for *gracilent* and *pudibund*. *You* might do something with that, but I lack inspiration.'

Page 105

1. The people who 'lean' and are 'leaning against' each other in lines 18 and 30 are reminiscent of *The Hollow Men* (1925).

2. *The Duchess of Malfi* by John Webster, III. ii. 69–70:

   You have cause to love me, I entered you into my heart
   Before you would vouchsafe to call for the keys.

Page 107

1. This is not a quotation from *Prufrock*, but another example of 'cadence reproduction'.

2. *The White Devil* by John Webster, III. ii. 331–3:

   What do the dead do, uncle? do they eat,
   Hear music, go a-hunting, and be merry,
   As we that live?

3. *The Duchess of Malfi*, III. ii. 67–8:

   When I wax gray, I shall have all the Court
   Powder their hair, with Arras, to be like me.

4. The Duchess and Antonio, formerly her steward, now her husband, are in her bed-chamber. She is brushing her hair, with her back to him, and for a joke he and the maid Cariola slip away unnoticed. She continues talking, and when there is no reply, turns with 'Have you lost your tongue?' to find that her brother Ferdinand, who is also her enemy, has been listening to her. Antonio and Cariola do not return until after he has left.

   Eliot remarked on the 'breathless tension' of this scene, and the poignancy of the Duchess's words, in a talk he gave on the Indian Service of the B.B.C., which was published in the *Listener*, xxvi. 675 (18 December 1941).

Page 109

1. Cf. lines 1–10 of this poem with the opening of Section V.

Page 111

1. This little poem was influenced by *The Bhagavad-Gītā* (with perhaps a nod to Emerson's *Brahma*).

   Cf. *The Bhagavad-Gītā*, ix. 16 (Trans. by R. C. Zaehner):

   I am the rite, the sacrifice,
   The offering for the dead, the healing herb:
   I am the sacred formula, the sacred butter am I,
   I am the fire, and I the oblation [offered in the fire].

   For the butter ('gheé') as used in sacrifice, see iv. 24.

Page 113

1. In 'An Anatomy of Melancholy' (*The Sewanee Review*, lxxiv. 1, Special Issue, Winter 1966) Mr. Conrad Aiken mentioned that he had 'long been familiar with such passages as "A woman drew her long black hair out tight"', which he 'had seen as poems or part-poems, in themselves. And now saw inserted into *The Waste Land* as into a mosaic.'

   It would seem from the handwriting that this poem, 'After the turning', and 'I am the Resurrection' were written about 1914 or even earlier.

Page 117

1. See *The Maid's Tragedy* by Beaumont and Fletcher.

   Deserted by her lover, Amintor, for Evadne, Aspatia disguises herself as her brother seeking to avenge his sister's wrong, and forces Amintor to kill her in a duel.

   Eliot quoted Aspatia's words as the epigraph to *Sweeney Erect* (1919):

   'And the trees about me
   Let them be dry and leafless; let the rocks
   Groan with continual surges; and behind me
   Make all a desolation. Look, look, wenches!'

2. Eliot returned to this image in *Difficulties of a Statesman* (1931):

   . . . the cyclamen spreads its wings . . .

Page 119

1. This is probably the third of the miscellaneous poems

rejected by Pound (the other two being *Song* and *Exequy*). 'One test is whether anything would be lacking, if the last three were omitted. I don't think it would.' (TWLC)

2. Bleistein first appears in *Burbank with a Baedeker: Bleistein with a Cigar* (1920):

> . . . But this or such was Bleistein's way:
> A saggy bending of the knees
> And elbows, with the palms turned out,
> Chicago Semite Viennese.
>
> A lustreless protrusive eye
> Stares from the protozoic slime
> At a perspective of Canaletto . . .

3. Graves' Disease is a synonym for exophthalmic goitre.

Cf. the use of lines from *The Tempest*, I. ii. 399–407.

Dirge was probably written in 1921.

(The original title of the 1920 poem was simply *Bleistein with a Cigar*, and the first draft has the following variants:

l. 2 Descending at a small hotel;] And Triton blew his wrinkled shell.
l. 6 Passed seaward with] Passed slowly like
l. 7 Slowly:] Seaward:
l. 29 the lion's wings] the lion's mane

'wings' is supplied in Pound's hand, and against 'shell' he has written: 'if you "hotel" this rhythm shd be weighted a bit, I think.')

Page 123

1. Probably an unconscious echo of *Othello*, I. iii. 94–5:

> . . . of spirit
> So still and quiet . . .

This poem may have been written in 1921.

THE WASTE LAND

Text of the First Edition

NEW YORK, BONI AND LIVERIGHT

1922

Nam Sibyllam quidem Cumis ego ipse oculis meis vidi in ampulla pendere, et cum illi pueri dicerent: *Σίβυλλα τί θέλεις;* respondebat illa: *ἀποθανεῖν θέλω.*

I. THE BURIAL OF THE DEAD

APRIL is the cruellest month, breeding
Lilacs out of the dead land, mixing
Memory and desire, stirring
Dull roots with spring rain.
Winter kept us warm, covering
Earth in forgetful snow, feeding
A little life with dried tubers.
Summer surprised us, coming over the Starnbergersee
With a shower of rain; we stopped in the colonnade,
And went on in sunlight, into the Hofgarten,
And drank coffee, and talked for an hour.
Bin gar keine Russin, stamm' aus Litauen, echt deutsch.
And when we were children, staying at the archduke's,
My cousin's, he took me out on a sled,
And I was frightened. He said, Marie,
Marie, hold on tight. And down we went.
In the mountains, there you feel free.
I read, much of the night, and go south in the winter.

What are the roots that clutch, what branches grow
Out of this stony rubbish? Son of man,
You cannot say, or guess, for you know only
A heap of broken images, where the sun beats,
And the dead tree gives no shelter, the cricket no relief,
And the dry stone no sound of water. Only
There is shadow under this red rock,
(Come in under the shadow of this red rock),
And I will show you something different from either
Your shadow at morning striding behind you
Or your shadow at evening rising to meet you;
I will show you fear in a handful of dust.

Frisch weht der Wind
Der Heimat zu.
Mein Irisch Kind,
Wo weilest du?

'You gave me hyacinths first a year ago;
'They called me the hyacinth girl.'

—Yet when we came back, late, from the Hyacinth garden,
Your arms full, and your hair wet, I could not
Speak, and my eyes failed, I was neither
Living nor dead, and I knew nothing,
Looking into the heart of light, the silence.
Od' und leer das Meer.

Madame Sosostris, famous clairvoyante,
Had a bad cold, nevertheless
Is known to be the wisest woman in Europe,
With a wicked pack of cards. Here, said she,
Is your card, the drowned Phoenician Sailor,
(Those are pearls that were his eyes. Look!)
Here is Belladonna, the Lady of the Rocks,
The lady of situations.
Here is the man with three staves, and here the Wheel,
And here is the one-eyed merchant, and this card,
Which is blank, is something he carries on his back,
Which I am forbidden to see. I do not find
The Hanged Man. Fear death by water.
I see crowds of people, walking round in a ring.
Thank you. If you see dear Mrs. Equitone,
Tell her I bring the horoscope myself:
One must be so careful these days.

Unreal City,
Under the brown fog of a winter dawn,
A crowd flowed over London Bridge, so many,
I had not thought death had undone so many.
Sighs, short and infrequent, were exhaled,
And each man fixed his eyes before his feet.
Flowed up the hill and down King William Street,
To where Saint Mary Woolnoth kept the hours
With a dead sound on the final stroke of nine.
There I saw one I knew, and stopped him, crying 'Stetson!
'You who were with me in the ships at Mylae!
'That corpse you planted last year in your garden,
'Has it begun to sprout? Will it bloom this year?
'Or has the sudden frost disturbed its bed?

Line 42 Od'] Oed'—Editor.

'Oh keep the Dog far hence, that's friend to men,
'Or with his nails he'll dig it up again!
'You! hypocrite lecteur!—mon semblable,—mon frère!'

II. A GAME OF CHESS

THE Chair she sat in, like a burnished throne,
Glowed on the marble, where the glass
Held up by standards wrought with fruited vines
From which a golden Cupidon peeped out
(Another hid his eyes behind his wing)
Doubled the flames of sevenbranched candelabra
Reflecting light upon the table as
The glitter of her jewels rose to meet it,
From satin cases poured in rich profusion;
In vials of ivory and coloured glass
Unstoppered, lurked her strange synthetic perfumes,
Unguent, powdered, or liquid—troubled, confused
And drowned the sense in odours; stirred by the air
That freshened from the window, these ascended
In fattening the prolonged candle-flames,
Flung their smoke into the laquearia,
Stirring the pattern on the coffered ceiling.
Huge sea-wood fed with copper
Burned green and orange, framed by the coloured stone,
In which sad light a carvèd dolphin swam.
Above the antique mantel was displayed
As though a window gave upon the sylvan scene
The change of Philomel, by the barbarous king
So rudely forced; yet there the nightingale
Filled all the desert with inviolable voice
And still she cried, and still the world pursues,
'Jug Jug' to dirty ears.
And other withered stumps of time
Were told upon the walls; staring forms
Leaned out, leaning, hushing the room enclosed.
Footsteps shuffled on the stair.
Under the firelight, under the brush, her hair
Spread out in fiery points
Glowed into words, then would be savagely still.

'My nerves are bad to-night. Yes, bad. Stay with me.
'Speak to me. Why do you never speak? Speak.
'What are you thinking of? What thinking? What?
'I never know what you are thinking. Think.'

I think we are in rats' alley
Where the dead men lost their bones.

'What is that noise?'
                                        The wind under the door.
'What is that noise now? What is the wind doing?'
                                        Nothing again nothing.
                                                                                    'Do
'You know nothing? Do you see nothing? Do you remember
'Nothing?'
    I remember
Those are pearls that were his eyes.
'Are you alive, or not? Is there nothing in your head?'
                                                                                                    But
O O O O that Shakespeherian Rag—
It's so elegant
So intelligent
'What shall I do now? What shall I do?'
'I shall rush out as I am, and walk the street
'With my hair down, so. What shall we do to-morrow?
'What shall we ever do?'
                                                The hot water at ten.
And if it rains, a closed car at four.
And we shall play a game of chess,
Pressing lidless eyes and waiting for a knock upon the door.

When Lil's husband got demobbed, I said—
I didn't mince my words, I said to her myself,
HURRY UP PLEASE IT'S TIME
Now Albert's coming back, make yourself a bit smart.
He'll want to know what you done with that money he gave you
To get yourself some teeth. He did, I was there.
You have them all out, Lil, and get a nice set,
He said, I swear, I can't bear to look at you.
And no more can't I, I said, and think of poor Albert,
He's been in the army four years, he wants a good time,

And if you don't give it him, there's others will, I said.
Oh is there, she said. Something o' that, I said.
Then I'll know who to thank, she said, and give me a straight look.
HURRY UP PLEASE IT'S TIME
If you don't like it you can get on with it, I said.
Others can pick and choose if you can't.
But if Albert makes off, it won't be for lack of telling.
You ought to be ashamed, I said, to look so antique.
(And her only thirty-one.)
I can't help it, she said, pulling a long face,
It's them pills I took, to bring it off, she said.
(She's had five already, and nearly died of young George.)
The chemist said it would be alright, but I've never been the same.
You *are* a proper fool, I said.
Well, if Albert won't leave you alone, there it is, I said,
What you get married for if you don't want children?
HURRY UP PLEASE IT'S TIME
Well, that Sunday Albert was home, they had a hot gammon,
And they asked me in to dinner, to get the beauty of it hot—
HURRY UP PLEASE IT'S TIME
HURRY UP PLEASE IT'S TIME
Goonight Bill. Goonight Lou. Goonight May. Goonight.
Ta ta. Goonight. Goonight.
Good night, ladies, good night, sweet ladies, good night, good night.

III. THE FIRE SERMON

THE river's tent is broken: the last fingers of leaf
Clutch and sink into the wet bank. The wind
Crosses the brown land, unheard. The nymphs are departed.
Sweet Thames, run softly, till I end my song.
The river bears no empty bottles, sandwich papers,
Silk handkerchiefs, cardboard boxes, cigarette ends
Or other testimony of summer nights. The nymphs are departed.
And their friends, the loitering heirs of city directors;
Departed, have left no addresses.

Line 161 *alright*. This spelling occurs also in the Hogarth Press edition—Editor.

By the waters of Leman I sat down and wept . . .
Sweet Thames, run softly till I end my song,
Sweet Thames, run softly, for I speak not loud or long.
But at my back in a cold blast I hear
The rattle of the bones, and chuckle spread from ear to ear.

A rat crept softly through the vegetation
Dragging its slimy belly on the bank
While I was fishing in the dull canal
On a winter evening round behind the gashouse
Musing upon the king my brother's wreck
And on the king my father's death before him.
White bodies naked on the low damp ground
And bones cast in a little low dry garret,
Rattled by the rat's foot only, year to year.
But at my back from time to time I hear
The sound of horns and motors, which shall bring
Sweeney to Mrs. Porter in the spring.
O the moon shone bright on Mrs. Porter
And on her daughter
They wash their feet in soda water
Et, O ces voix d'enfants, chantant dans la coupole!

Twit twit twit
Jug jug jug jug jug jug
So rudely forc'd.
Tereu

Unreal City
Under the brown fog of a winter noon
Mr. Eugenides, the Smyrna merchant
Unshaven, with a pocket full of currants
C.i.f. London: documents at sight,
Asked me in demotic French
To luncheon at the Cannon Street Hotel
Followed by a weekend at the Metropole.

At the violet hour, when the eyes and back
Turn upward from the desk, when the human engine waits
Like a taxi throbbing waiting,
I Tiresias, though blind, throbbing between two lives,
Old man with wrinkled female breasts, can see

At the violet hour, the evening hour that strives
Homeward, and brings the sailor home from sea,
The typist home at teatime, clears her breakfast, lights
Her stove, and lays out food in tins.
Out of the window perilously spread
Her drying combinations touched by the sun's last rays,
On the divan are piled (at night her bed)
Stockings, slippers, camisoles, and stays.
I Tiresias, old man with wrinkled dugs
Perceived the scene, and foretold the rest—
I too awaited the expected guest.
He, the young man carbuncular, arrives,
A small house agent's clerk, with one bold stare,
One of the low on whom assurance sits
As a silk hat on a Bradford millionaire.
The time is now propitious, as he guesses,
The meal is ended, she is bored and tired,
Endeavours to engage her in caresses
Which still are unreproved, if undesired.
Flushed and decided, he assaults at once;
Exploring hands encounter no defence;
His vanity requires no response,
And makes a welcome of indifference.
(And I Tiresias have foresuffered all
Enacted on this same divan or bed;
I who have sat by Thebes below the wall
And walked among the lowest of the dead.)
Bestows one final patronising kiss,
And gropes his way, finding the stairs unlit . . .

She turns and looks a moment in the glass,
Hardly aware of her departed lover;
Her brain allows one half-formed thought to pass:
'Well now that's done: and I'm glad it's over.'
When lovely woman stoops to folly and
Paces about her room again, alone,
She smoothes her hair with automatic hand,
And puts a record on the gramophone.

'This music crept by me upon the waters'
And along the Strand, up Queen Victoria Street.

O City city, I can sometimes hear
Beside a public bar in Lower Thames Street,
The pleasant whining of a mandoline
And a clatter and a chatter from within
Where fishmen lounge at noon: where the walls
Of Magnus Martyr hold
Inexplicable splendour of Ionian white and gold.

The river sweats
Oil and tar
The barges drift
With the turning tide
Red sails
Wide
To leeward, swing on the heavy spar.
The barges wash
Drifting logs
Down Greenwich reach
Past the Isle of Dogs.
Weialala leia
Wallala leialala

Elizabeth and Leicester
Beating oars
The stern was formed
A gilded shell
Red and gold
The brisk swell
Rippled both shores
Southwest wind
Carried down stream
The peal of bells
White towers
Weialala leia
Wallala leialala

'Trams and dusty trees.
Highbury bore me. Richmond and Kew
Undid me. By Richmond I raised my knees
Supine on the floor of a narrow canoe.'

'My feet are at Moorgate, and my heart
Under my feet. After the event
He wept. He promised "a new start".
I made no comment. What should I resent?'
'On Margate Sands.
I can connect
Nothing with nothing.
The broken fingernails of dirty hands.
My people humble people who expect
Nothing.'

la la

To Carthage then I came

Burning burning burning burning
O Lord Thou pluckest me out
O Lord Thou pluckest

burning

IV. DEATH BY WATER

PHLEBAS the Phoenician, a fortnight dead,
Forgot the cry of gulls, and the deep sea swell
And the profit and loss.
A current under sea
Picked his bones in whispers. As he rose and fell
He passed the stages of his age and youth
Entering the whirlpool.
Gentile or Jew
O you who turn the wheel and look to windward,
Consider Phlebas, who was once handsome and tall as you.

V. WHAT THE THUNDER SAID

AFTER the torchlight red on sweaty faces
After the frosty silence in the gardens
After the agony in stony places
The shouting and the crying
Prison and palace and reverberation
Of thunder of spring over distant mountains

He who was living is now dead
We who were living are now dying
With a little patience

Here is no water but only rock
Rock and no water and the sandy road
The road winding above among the mountains
Which are mountains of rock without water
If there were water we should stop and drink
Amongst the rock one cannot stop or think
Sweat is dry and feet are in the sand
If there were only water amongst the rock
Dead mountain mouth of carious teeth that cannot spit
Here one can neither stand nor lie nor sit
There is not even silence in the mountains
But dry sterile thunder without rain
There is not even solitude in the mountains
But red sullen faces sneer and snarl
From doors of mudcracked houses
                                                  If there were water
    And no rock
    If there were rock
    And also water
    And water
    A spring
    A pool among the rock
    If there were the sound of water only
    Not the cicada
    And dry grass singing
    But sound of water over a rock
    Where the hermit-thrush sings in the pine trees
    Drip drop drip drop drop drop drop
    But there is no water

Who is the third who walks always beside you?
When I count, there are only you and I together
But when I look ahead up the white road
There is always another one walking beside you
Gliding wrapt in a brown mantle, hooded
I do not know whether a man or a woman
—But who is that on the other side of you?

What is that sound high in the air
Murmur of maternal lamentation
Who are those hooded hordes swarming
Over endless plains, stumbling in cracked earth
Ringed by the flat horizon only
What is the city over the mountains
Cracks and reforms and bursts in the violet air
Falling towers
Jerusalem Athens Alexandria
Vienna London
Unreal

A woman drew her long black hair out tight
And fiddled whisper music on those strings
And bats with baby faces in the violet light
Whistled, and beat their wings
And crawled head downward down a blackened wall
And upside down in air were towers
Tolling reminiscent bells, that kept the hours
And voices singing out of empty cisterns and exhausted wells.

In this decayed hole among the mountains
In the faint moonlight, the grass is singing
Over the tumbled graves, about the chapel
There is the empty chapel, only the wind's home.
It has no windows, and the door swings,
Dry bones can harm no one.
Only a cock stood on the rooftree
Co co rico co co rico
In a flash of lightning. Then a damp gust
Bringing rain

Ganga was sunken, and the limp leaves
Waited for rain, while the black clouds
Gathered far distant, over Himavant.
The jungle crouched, humped in silence.
Then spoke the thunder
DA
Datta: what have we given?
My friend, blood shaking my heart
The awful daring of a moment's surrender

Which an age of prudence can never retract
By this, and this only, we have existed
Which is not to be found in our obituaries
Or in memories draped by the beneficent spider
Or under seals broken by the lean solicitor
In our empty rooms
DA
Dayadhvam: I have heard the key
Turn in the door once and turn once only
We think of the key, each in his prison
Thinking of the key, each confirms a prison
Only at nightfall, aetherial rumours
Revive for a moment a broken Coriolanus
DA
Damyata: The boat responded
Gaily, to the hand expert with sail and oar
The sea was calm, your heart would have responded
Gaily, when invited, beating obedient
To controlling hands

I sat upon the shore
Fishing, with the arid plain behind me
Shall I at least set my lands in order?

London Bridge is falling down falling down falling down

Poi s'ascose nel foco che gli affina
Quando fiam ceu chelidon—O swallow swallow
Le Prince d'Aquitaine à la tour abolie
These fragments I have shored against my ruins
Why then Ile fit you. Hieronymo's mad againe.
Datta. Dayadhvam. Damyata.

Shantih shantih shantih

Line 415 aetherial] aethereal
Line 428 ceu] uti—Editor

NOTES

Not only the title, but the plan and a good deal of the incidental symbolism of the poem were suggested by Miss Jessie L. Weston's book on the Grail legend: *From Ritual to Romance* (Macmillan).[1] Indeed, so deeply am I indebted, Miss Weston's book will elucidate the difficulties of the poem much better than my notes can do; and I recommend it (apart from the great interest of the book itself) to any who think such elucidation of the poem worth the trouble. To another work of anthropology I am indebted in general, one which has influenced our generation profoundly; I mean *The Golden Bough*; I have used especially the two volumes *Adonis, Attis, Osiris*. Anyone who is acquainted with these works will immediately recognize in the poem certain references to vegetation ceremonies.

I. THE BURIAL OF THE DEAD

Line 20. Cf. Ezekiel 2:7.

23. Cf. Ecclesiastes 12:5.

31. *V. Tristan und Isolde*, i, verses 5–8.

42. Id. iii, verse 24.

46. I am not familiar with the exact constitution of the Tarot pack of cards, from which I have obviously departed to suit my own convenience. The Hanged Man, a member of the traditional pack, fits my purpose in two ways: because he is associated in my mind with the Hanged God of Frazer, and because I associate him with the hooded figure in the passage of the disciples to Emmaus in Part V. The Phoenician Sailor and the Merchant appear later; also the 'crowds of people', and Death by Water is executed in Part IV. The Man with Three Staves (an authentic member of the Tarot pack) I associate, quite arbitrarily, with the Fisher King himself.

60. Cf. Baudelaire:

> Fourmillante cité, cité pleine de rêves,
> Où le spectre en plein jour raccroche le passant.

63. Cf. *Inferno*, iii. 55–7:

> si lunga tratta
> di gente, ch'io non avrei mai creduto
> che morte tanta n'avesse disfatta.

64. Cf. *Inferno*, iv. 25–7:

> Quivi, secondo che per ascoltare,
> non avea pianto, ma' che di sospiri,
> che l'aura eterna facevan tremare.

68. A phenomenon which I have often noticed.

74. Cf. the Dirge in Webster's *White Devil*.

76. *V.* Baudelaire, Preface to *Fleurs du Mal*.

II. A GAME OF CHESS

77. Cf. *Antony and Cleopatra*, II. ii. 190.

92. Laquearia. *V. Aeneid*, I. 726:

> dependent lychni laquearibus aureis incensi, et noctem flammis
> funalia vincunt.

98. Sylvan scene. *V.* Milton, *Paradise Lost*, iv. 140.

99. *V.* Ovid, *Metamorphoses*, vi, Philomela.

100. Cf. Part III, l. 204.

115. Cf. Part III, l. 195.

118. Cf. Webster: 'Is the wind in that door still?'

126. Cf. Part I, l. 37, 48.

138. Cf. the game of chess in Middleton's *Women beware Women*.

III. THE FIRE SERMON

176. *V.* Spenser, *Prothalamion*.

192. Cf. *The Tempest*, I. ii.

196. Cf. Marvell, *To His Coy Mistress*.

197. Cf. Day, *Parliament of Bees*:

> When of the sudden, listening, you shall hear,
> A noise of horns and hunting, which shall bring
> Actaeon to Diana in the spring,
> Where all shall see her naked skin . . .

199. I do not know the origin of the ballad from which these lines are taken: it was reported to me from Sydney, Australia.

202. *V.* Verlaine, *Parsifal*.

210. The currants were quoted at a price 'carriage and insurance free to London'; and the Bill of Lading, etc.,

[1] Macmillan] Cambridge.

Notes 196 and 197 were transposed in this and the Hogarth Press edition, but have been corrected here. 210. 'Carriage and insurance free'] 'cost, insurance and freight'—Editor.

were to be handed to the buyer upon payment of the sight draft.

218. Tiresias, although a mere spectator and not indeed a 'character', is yet the most important personage in the poem, uniting all the rest. Just as the one-eyed merchant, seller of currants, melts into the Phoenician Sailor, and the latter is not wholly distinct from Ferdinand Prince of Naples, so all the women are one woman, and the two sexes meet in Tiresias. What Tiresias *sees*, in fact, is the substance of the poem. The whole passage from Ovid is of great anthropological interest:

> . . . Cum Iunone iocos et 'maior vestra profecto est
> Quam, quae contingit maribus', dixisse, 'voluptas.'
> Illa negat; placuit quae sit sententia docti
> Quaerere Tiresiae: venus huic erat utraque nota.
> Nam duo magnorum viridi coeuntia silva
> Corpora serpentum baculi violaverat ictu
> Deque viro factus, mirabile, femina septem
> Egerat autumnos; octavo rursus eosdem
> Vidit et 'est vestrae si tanta potentia plagae',
> Dixit 'ut auctoris sortem in contraria mutet,
> Nunc quoque vos feriam!' percussis anguibus isdem
> Forma prior rediit genetivaque venit imago.
> Arbiter hic igitur sumptus de lite iocosa
> Dicta Iovis firmat; gravius Saturnia iusto
> Nec pro materia fertur doluisse suique
> Iudicis aeterna damnavit lumina nocte,
> At pater omnipotens (neque enim licet inrita cuiquam
> Facta dei fecisse deo) pro lumine adempto
> Scire futura dedit poenamque levavit honore.

221. This may not appear as exact as Sappho's lines, but I had in mind the 'longshore' or 'dory' fisherman, who returns at nightfall.

253. *V.* Goldsmith, the song in *The Vicar of Wakefield.*

257. *V. The Tempest*, as above.

264. The interior of St. Magnus Martyr is to my mind one of the finest among Wren's interiors. See *The Proposed Demolition of Nineteen City Churches* (P. S. King & Son, Ltd.).

266. The Song of the (three) Thames-daughters begins here. From line 292 to 306 inclusive they speak in turn. *V. Götterdämmerung*, III. i: the Rhine-daughters.

279. *V.* Froude, *Elizabeth*, vol. I, ch. iv, letter of De Quadra to Philip of Spain:

> In the afternoon we were in a barge, watching the games on the river. (The queen) was alone with Lord Robert and myself on the poop, when they began to talk nonsense, and went so far that Lord Robert at last said, as I was on the spot there was no reason why they should not be married if the queen pleased.

293. Cf. *Purgatorio*, v. 133:

> 'Ricorditi di me, che son la Pia;
> Siena mi fe', disfecemi Maremma.'

307. *V.* St. Augustine's *Confessions*: 'to Carthage then I came, where a cauldron of unholy loves sang all about mine ears'.

308. The complete text of the Buddha's Fire Sermon (which corresponds in importance to the Sermon on the Mount) from which these words are taken, will be found translated in the late Henry Clarke Warren's *Buddhism in Translation* (Harvard Oriental Series). Mr. Warren was one of the great pioneers of Buddhist studies in the Occident.

309. From St. Augustine's *Confessions* again. The collocation of these two representatives of eastern and western asceticism, as the culmination of this part of the poem, is not an accident.

V. WHAT THE THUNDER SAID

In the first part of Part V three themes are employed: the journey to Emmaus, the approach to the Chapel Perilous (see Miss Weston's book), and the present decay of eastern Europe.

357. This is *Turdus aonalaschkae pallasii*, the hermit-thrush which I have heard in Quebec County. Chapman says (*Handbook of Birds of Eastern North America*) 'it is most at home in secluded woodland and thickety retreats. . . . Its notes are not remarkable for variety or volume, but in purity and sweetness of tone and exquisite modulation they are unequalled.' Its 'water-dripping song' is justly celebrated.

360. The following lines were stimulated by the account of one of the Antarctic expeditions (I forget which, but I think one of Shackleton's): it was related that the party of explorers, at the extremity of their strength, had the constant delusion that there was *one more member* than could actually be counted.

366–76. Cf. Hermann Hesse, *Blick ins Chaos*:

> Schon ist halb Europa, schon ist zumindest der halbe Osten Europas auf dem Wege zum Chaos, fährt betrunken im heiligen Wahn am Abgrund entlang und singt dazu, singt betrunken und hymnisch wie Dmitri Karamasoff sang. Ueber diese Lieder lacht der Bürger beleidigt, der Heilige und Seher hört sie mit Tränen.

401. 'Datta, dayadhvam, damyata' (Give, sympathize, control). The fable of the meaning of the Thunder is found in the *Brihadaranyaka—Upanishad*, 5, I. A translation is found in Deussen's *Sechzig Upanishads des Veda*, p. 489.

407. Cf. Webster, *The White Devil*, v. vi:

> . . . they'll remarry
> Ere the worm pierce your winding-sheet, ere the spider
> Make a thin curtain for your epitaphs.

411. Cf. *Inferno*, xxxiii. 46:

> ed io sentii chiavar l'uscio di sotto
> all'orribile torre.

Also F. H. Bradley, *Appearance and Reality*, p. 346:

> My external sensations are no less private to myself than are my thoughts or my feelings. In either case my experience falls within my own circle, a circle closed on the outside; and, with all its elements alike, every sphere is opaque to the others which surround it. . . . In brief, regarded as an existence which appears in a soul, the whole world for each is peculiar and private to that soul.

424. *V.* Weston, *From Ritual to Romance*; chapter on the Fisher King.

427. *V. Purgatorio*, xxvi. 148.

> 'Ara vos prec per aquella valor
> 'que vos guida al som de l'escalina,
> 'sovegna vos a temps de ma dolor.'
> Poi s'ascose nel foco che gli affina.

428. *V. Pervigilium Veneris.* Cf. Philomela in Parts II and III.

429. *V.* Gerard de Nerval, Sonnet *El Desdichado.*

431. *V.* Kyd's *Spanish Tragedy.*

433. Shantih. Repeated as here, a formal ending to an Upanishad. 'The Peace which passeth understanding' is a feeble translation of the content of this word.